CENTRE FOR EDUCATIONAL RESEARCH AND INNOVATION

INNOVATING
SCHOOLS

ORGANISATION FOR ECONOMIC CO-OPERATION AND DEVELOPMENT

ORGANISATION FOR ECONOMIC CO-OPERATION AND DEVELOPMENT

Pursuant to Article 1 of the Convention signed in Paris on 14th December 1960, and which came into force on 30th September 1961, the Organisation for Economic Co-operation and Development (OECD) shall promote policies designed:

- to achieve the highest sustainable economic growth and employment and a rising standard of living in Member countries, while maintaining financial stability, and thus to contribute to the development of the world economy;
- to contribute to sound economic expansion in Member as well as non-member countries in the process of economic development; and
- to contribute to the expansion of world trade on a multilateral, non-discriminatory basis in accordance with international obligations.

The original Member countries of the OECD are Austria, Belgium, Canada, Denmark, France, Germany, Greece, Iceland, Ireland, Italy, Luxembourg, the Netherlands, Norway, Portugal, Spain, Sweden, Switzerland, Turkey, the United Kingdom and the United States. The following countries became Members subsequently through accession at the dates indicated hereafter: Japan (28th April 1964), Finland (28th January 1969), Australia (7th June 1971), New Zealand (29th May 1973), Mexico (18th May 1994), the Czech Republic (21st December 1995), Hungary (7th May 1996), Poland (22nd November 1996) and Korea (12th December 1996). The Commission of the European Communities takes part in the work of the OECD (Article 13 of the OECD Convention).

The Centre for Educational Research and Innovation was created in June 1968 by the Council of the Organisation for Economic Co-operation and Development and all Member countries of the OECD are participants.

The main objectives of the Centre are as follows:

- *analyse and develop research, innovation and key indicators in current and emerging education and learning issues, and their links to other sectors of policy;*
- *explore forward-looking coherent approaches to education and learning in the context of national and international cultural, social and economic change; and*
- *facilitate practical co-operation among Member countries and, where relevant, with non-member countries, in order to seek solutions and exchange views of educational problems of common interest.*

The Centre functions within the Organisation for Economic Co-operation and Development in accordance with the decisions of the Council of the Organisation, under the authority of the Secretary-General. It is supervised by a Governing Board composed of one national expert in its field of competence from each of the countries participating in its programme of work.

Publié en français sous le titre :
LES ÉCOLES INNOVANTES

Foreword

"Schooling for tomorrow" has emerged as a key CERI project area informing OECD's educational thinking. Work on this project began in 1997, and the first main event was an international seminar held in Hiroshima University, Japan, 5-7 November 1997. This volume brings together the main papers and results from that conference.

The seminar was organised by CERI/OECD and *Monbusho* (the Japanese Ministry for Education, Science, Sports and Culture), with the University of Hiroshima and Hiroshima Prefecture. It was the sixth in a series of OECD/Japan seminars held annually on a matter of high policy or research interest in education.[1] It was by far the largest of the seminars organised to date in this series: around 60 national experts and other specialists, Japanese government and OECD staff, drawn from 24 countries gathered in Hiroshima University. They were joined, in addition, by the "virtual conference" – the electronic discussion group of educators and analysts from around the world, exchanging ideas and reactions before and during the event in Hiroshima.

Within the OECD/CERI context, the agenda for change arises in large part from the pressing need for schools to contribute fully to fulfilling the goal of "lifelong learning for all". This goal was clearly stated in the Ministers of Education's meeting in Paris in 1996 (OECD, 1996). The ministers set the parameters for new CERI work when they expressed concern about "education systems' capacity to change quickly,

---

1. The five previous seminars were: "Teacher Education and the Quality of Schooling" (February 1993); "Massification of Higher Education: Financing and Innovation" (March 1994); "Lifelong Learning: A Strategy for the Future" (June 1994); "Integrated Learning and Transition from School to Work" (November 1995); "Changing the Subject: Innovation in Science and Mathematics Education" (November 1996). The OECD/Japan education seminars have a dual purpose. First, they permit Japanese experiences and innovations to be brought more fully into OECD and international reflections on subjects of wide educational interest. Second, they make an important contribution to the work of OECD through the hosting by the Japanese authorities of an annual conference of practitioners, experts and policy-makers on a subject of interest both to Japan and the OECD.

at a time when many factors are combining to influence the shape of tomorrow's schools". In particular, existing ways of organising education need to be rethought, they concluded, to remove rigidities and enhance the incentives for both children and adults to learn. Ministers invited the OECD to: "assess alternative visions of the 'school of tomorrow', in particular in the light of new technologies and advances in pedagogy" (*op. cit.*, p. 22).

From these aims, two main perspectives on schooling for the future provided the focus for the seminar and this volume, set in the context of the broader trends and policy developments: the exchange and analysis of concrete examples and initiatives, on the one hand, and debate on the nature of innovation, on the other. Japan provided a natural setting to address these issues. It has a school system that is widely viewed with envy in other countries, because, for instance, of the standards achieved by many of its students, especially in the mathematics and science fields, and the high public regard which education enjoys. Such achievements notwithstanding, for more than a decade, there has been a series of reform endeavours, including on-going reforms to prepare the next generation for the 21st century. These have sought to address perceived problems: reducing the intensive competition in Japanese school education while augmenting individualism and creativity in the curriculum; promoting international understanding; addressing problems associated with school violence and bullying. Over approximately the same period, lifelong learning has become prominent in Japan, commonly understood more as a concept for individual and cultural promotion than the strong economic and social rationale given to lifelong learning in many other OECD countries.

The introduction prepared by David Istance for the OECD/CERI Secretariat reflects the broad concern that schools should lay the foundation for lifelong learning and identifies a selection of the main questions that guided the conference discussion.

The key addresses are contained in Parts I, II and III, focusing on issues of curriculum, innovation, and school structures.[2] All these chapters, in their different ways, address the broader context in which schools in OECD countries find themselves going into the 21st century and the extent to which this defines new challenges, as well addressing continuity (that Hutmacher in particular reflects on). They draw on experiences, traditions and literatures from very different systems and world regions. Part I places the debate on schooling for tomorrow in the light both of future challenges for, present functions, and past experience in terms of what schools actually achieve. The chapters are written by Kerry J. Kennedy, of the University of Canberra, Australia, and Walo Hutmacher, of the University of Geneva, Switzerland. Part II focuses on the innovation issue with chapters by David H. Hargreaves, of the

---

2. The paper by Cros was prepared in French and not presented to the seminar, while she was one of the French national representatives at Hiroshima.

University of Cambridge, the United Kingdom; Francoise Cros, of the Institut national de recherche pédagogique, Paris, France. Part III brings together policies and perspectives from Japan based on two contributions: by Tomiji Sugawa, Director of the Upper Secondary School Division, *Monbusho*, Japan, on the specific aims of recent school reforms,[3] and by Akira Ninomiya, University of Hiroshima, Japan, with his vision for the school of tomorrow.

The conference rapporteur, Donald Hirsch, has drawn together in the conclusions ideas from all the discussions, not only of the main seminar in Hiroshima but also of the electronic "virtual conference" seminar that took place alongside the "face-to-face" debate in Japan.

These chapters are complemented by the documentary basis for the seminar provided by national cases of innovative schools and schooling, specifically requested and submitted, and synthesised as an appendix. The cases were to be both innovative and exemplary, leaving it open as to whether they were of individual school institutions/learning centres, or instead of clusters of such institutions in a network or subsystem of schools. They could be either or both those that have moved well towards becoming "learning organisations", using a range of innovative methods, practices or technologies in new combinations, or those which have recast their relationships with their wider community in a significant way, recognising that the relevant "community" can vary very widely. By reproducing many extracts from the case material, these experiences are described largely in the words of the schools themselves.

As the outcome of one of the OECD/Japan education seminars, this publication has depended on the active involvement of many: in Japan, within the OECD Secretariat, as well as through the participants in the conference discussions themselves. The success of the conference depended particularly on the energies of the officials in the Japanese Ministry of Education, Science, Sports and Culture (*Monbusho*) and of Professor Ninomiya and his colleagues at Hiroshima University. Within the OECD Secretariat, David Istance of the Centre for Educational Research and Innovation was principally responsible for preparation of the publication. It is published on the responsibility of the Secretary-General.

---

3. This is based on his own selection of developments in Japan rather than as an official statement.

OECD 1999

Table of Contents

Introduction

Schooling for Tomorrow and Lifelong Learning

by

David Istance
OECD Secretariat

The OECD Secretariat (David Istance) provides an introduction to the background and questions that are influential in OECD thinking. Schooling for tomorrow is placed firmly in the lifelong learning context, but the picture is mixed as regards progress towards lifelong learning, calling for more systematic attention to how initial education can contribute to this broad aim. The chapter formulates some guiding questions, many of which are reflected and addressed in subsequent chapters. These include questions about the nature of innovation in schooling, its relation to the broader goals and developments in education and to national reform initiatives, and the more general relationships and tensions between reform and innovation.

Background and approaches

The new OECD/CERI project on "schooling for tomorrow" derives directly from the issues identified as priorities for future OECD analysis by the Ministers of Education at their 1996 meeting in Paris. They invited the Organisation: "to assess alternative visions of the 'school of tomorrow', in particular in the light of new technologies and advances in pedagogy" and "to study promising approaches to the 'school of tomorrow' and identify examples of good practice for wider dissemination" (OECD, 1996, p. 22).

These ministerial invitations, and the widespread demand from many quarters to identify new pathways for educational development into the 21st century, were the inspiration behind this Hiroshima seminar. The focus on promising, innovative examples lies at its core. Having identified such cases does not mean, however, that the goals and the means to implement them are already agreed by all, or that desired change will automatically follow elsewhere on the basis of the promising models. The process of innovation needs to be examined in its own right. Issues of the distribution of learning opportunities and the implementation of educational change, placed in the large context of social, economic and international currents, inform the understanding of the particular examples. Addressing these broader questions provides the complementary focus to the compilation and discussion of the innovative cases.

There is no single line of development or methodological stance that monopolises our understanding of schooling for tomorrow; we may approach it from different angles. We may adopt a focus that is *normative* – seeking to create particular "tomorrows". We may instead take a more detached *analytical* approach – elaborating implications about the future on an empirical basis. Whichever is the dominant approach, consideration of the future is coloured by its inherent uncertainty, blurring the lines between prediction and prescription. There are also differences depending on the levels under scrutiny – from micro developments in individual schools, classes or initiatives (as presented in the national examples prepared for this seminar) through to macro systems, national and international; from specific key aspects (such as use of technology or organisation) to the whole picture. Moreover, ideological viewpoints differ. So, there is a variety of viewpoints on the extent to which schools should be geared to serve various economic, social and cultural demands – and *which* ones? – or instead be largely free of external pressures, as some educators would argue. There are thus competing views, and with these a variety of tensions.

Tensions exist (further explored in this volume) between reforming systems through "macro" education policy instruments and fostering innovation at the grass roots. And, among those reforms that are being implemented may be detected a certain ambiguity as regards the school as an institution, for while some reforms seek to strengthen schools as dynamic organisations with powerful identities and ethos, others may weaken them through extending alternatives to move towards a measure of "de-schooling". In the midst of the variety of the viewpoints and tensions in play, it certainly cannot be assumed that the pathways for the future are to be revealed in the official statements of government policy. Such statements contain important pointers to national policy perceptions regarding the future for schooling in the 21st century, but such visions can only ever be partial. Governments are not omnipotent and their influence is circumscribed by other spheres – parental demand, the media, decentralised and sometimes "deschooled" learning arrangements, social and economic circumstances. Learning takes place in many ways and settings that lie outside schools *per se*. All these different viewpoints, approaches and stakeholders should be entered into our reflections on the future of schooling.

Schooling for lifelong learning

Lifelong learning is now the broad aim that commands widespread consensus as the way ahead for education. International and national reports abound (including those produced by OECD), refining its rationale and interpretation. In the country cases of innovative schools submitted to the Hiroshima seminar (see Appendix), there are numerous references to the endeavours of particular schools to contribute to lifelong learning through seeking to improve their students' abilities and motivation to become autonomous learners. Lifelong learning is an idea powerful in its simplicity. Learning – formal, non-formal, and informal – should be a lifetime matter. It cannot be confined to the early years of infancy, childhood and adolescence. Old models of elementary schooling, followed up with apprenticeships for some, and universities for still fewer – all primarily experienced by the young – were never adequate for the 20th century, and still less so for the 21st. It is, however, much more difficult to agree on what are the specific aims of learning to be accorded priority or the strategies needed to put lifelong learning in place than it is to advocate the broad aim. In many cases, rhetoric and reality are still far apart.

To include schooling so prominently in the lifelong learning equation represents a relatively recent consensus. Not very long ago, lifelong learning was widely regarded as something relevant primarily for adults, leaving schools largely untouched. Over time, however, it has become clearer that schooling should be regarded as an integral element of the whole enterprise if our perspective is to be genuinely lifelong. Particular strategies to implement the broad aim will then need to incorporate consideration of the extent to which initial schooling provides or not a sound foundation to all young people for their subsequent learning and life more generally. Again, however, reality may not have caught up with the rhetoric. Noting the shifting parameters of consensus in policy documents is very different from observing new lifelong learning practices becoming firmly embedded in schools.

There is also mixed evidence regarding the extent to which the broad trends of participation can be characterised as amounting to the strengthening of the lifelong learning model. On the positive side of the mixed picture, there has been an enormous flourishing of learning by older people and adults in a whole variety of forms. Lifelong learning has or is becoming a reality for many. On the other side, the front-end system of education for the young, far from loosening its grip as some have maintained to be a prerequisite of progress towards lifelong learning, appears to be moving from strength to strength. More stay on, not just in upper secondary education or training but in some form of tertiary education as well. Around four out of ten 20-year-olds in most OECD countries are now in education, and in a few this rises to half or more of this age group (CERI/OECD, 1997, Chapter C). Despite such large numbers of young people extending their initial education into the upper-secondary and tertiary cycles, demand is still not being satisfied so that recent OECD analyses (OECD, 1998) conclude that the forces at play can be expected to drive towards even higher levels of participation in tertiary education. Some of this will be in continuing programmes, but a large part will be to strengthen still further the initial, front-end system. It is just as possible to argue that more rigid age segmentation is setting in, with education the dominant life experience for many up to the age of 18, 20, 22 or 25 years of age, as to argue the opposite case that more flexible life patterns are becoming the norm.

Hence, we should not let our enthusiasm for the broad aim of implementing "lifelong learning for all" obscure the fact that this is far from secured. There have been extensive reforms of schooling across OECD countries, yet it is not obvious that these have been driven by the lifelong learning imperative. It is clear that there is a greater range of learnings and participation in them than there used to be in many countries, but there is far less clarity about the role of schools and schooling as a distinct early phase of the lifespan in laying the foundation for lifelong learning. Especially as the initial phase of education in becoming more and more protracted, it is time now to undertake a more fundamental re-think of what the role of schools should be as a distinct part of the lifelong panoply of learning. What should be the particular missions of schools? What to develop in partnerships, and what should be left to others? How to make the answers to these questions the defining aims of all schools, not just the most successful? Clarifying the responses to these questions represents a key part of clarifying "schooling for tomorrow".

Curriculum issues

The curriculum and its implementation lie at the heart of these questions. There is a widespread view (again as expressed in debates rather than necessarily reflected in practice) that the nature of learning and life skills required for the 21st century cut across traditional curriculum boundaries, requiring students to "learn how to learn" and to develop interpersonal, communication and problem-solving skills, as well as the ability actively to use new information and communication technologies. Strong links are needed between subject-based theoretical knowledge and its practical applications. The focus on competence and active approaches to learning should go hand in hand with mastery of subject matter, understanding and developing expertise. Traditional distinctions between, for instance, academic and vocational learning fit poorly into a dynamic, lifelong curriculum framework. All students need a wide repertoire of knowledge and skills, where the boundaries between preparation for employment and the other aims for learning (often characterised as social and developmental) become increasingly blurred. How to develop flexible curricula opening up individualised learning paths, yet which equip all with the essential competences and motivations to continue as lifelong learners? And, preparation for lifelong learning is about motivation and attitude, including towards new learning, that are as, perhaps even more, important as the acquisition of more tangible, discrete competences. How successfully, in this case, does schooling foster motivation, giving students a basis of identity and inclusion rather than contributing to alienation and exclusion? These, too, are key aspects of the new curricular and organisational challenges facing schools.

Despite an emerging policy consensus on many of these points across many OECD countries, there remain strong pressures that inhibit the development of curriculum and schooling consistently towards these principles. Parents and the public at large often expect schools to excel in traditional, familiar tasks rather than to experiment with new approaches, especially if they perceive a conflict between the concern that their children learn key "basics" and the adoption of new ambitious curricula, organisation or methods. Examinations, testing and assessment regimes that underpin qualifications and accountability policies exert powerful constraints on schools that wish to move towards more active learning and cross-curricular competences, pressures that, if anything, are increasing. There is the real question of how far schools and teachers themselves have developed the skills and expertise entailed by the move towards lifelong learning. And with the sheer volume and persistence of recent school reforms, an element of "fatigue" may have set in among those continually expected to embrace new changes. In sum, there are powerful tensions at play.

Convergence or divergence?

Because of international globalisation, in educational exchange and awareness as well as in economic and cultural life, it might be supposed that education and learning systems are being drawn together in a broad process of convergence. Shared strategies, such as the pursuit of lifelong learning, represent international as well as national agendas. Yet, the tensions referred to here may lead to different solutions emerging with the result that differences widen not narrow. The flexibility and individualisation inherent in the lifelong learning concept imply diversity not homogeneity. Today's "knowledge society" is placing an increasing premium on learning that may well cause differences in pathways and outcomes to be exacerbated, even while the pressures themselves are shared by all. In short, it might be mistaken to aim towards *the* school of tomorrow, if instead variety and diversity are on the increase. Whether the forces making for convergence or divergence prove to be more powerful must remain an open question.

Innovation and reform

The importance attached to innovation within the learning policy agenda itself implies a degree of openness to uncertainty and multiple, unpredictable solutions. It is common now to acknowledge that fundamental and effective changes in teaching practices and learning processes are best developed when schools are actively engaged in innovation and are able to exercise some freedom to experiment. Yet, as noted, there is a range of pressures that creates caution about experimentation or inhibits it altogether. In most countries, schools have acquired greater managerial autonomy, but this is still within powerful centrally-defined parameters about curriculum, performance, and funding that can prove every bit as constraining as formal regulation. National reforms aimed at generalising improvements can thus conflict with local innovation, whether found in individual schools or networks of schools. For instance, the priority of reforms may lead to school and teacher development activities being directed largely towards the incorporation of changed procedures or regulations, rather than to developing new practices (CERI/OECD, 1998*b*).

Certain key questions can help shape analysis and debate in clarifying schooling for the future, including:

- What are the characteristics of those schools that have been identified as among the most interesting innovative examples? Why should they be regarded as innovatory and why should their example be followed? What lessons have been learnt about the sustainability of innovation over time: can it be achieved? How dependent is innovation on particular or individual circumstances? How relevant is the size of the school?

- How fair is the criticism that there is no shortage of models for the future, but that many are relatively privileged elite examples realised under the combination of highly favourable factors? What happens when those ingredients are lacking – how much should we expect of the ordinary unexceptional school, quite apart from those weighed down with problems?

- Is there a tension between seeking change at the level of each individual school organisation, which is where many decisions have been decentralised to but which naturally affects only limited numbers of students, and developing models that operate through networks or "sub-systems" of schools? How extensive is our knowledge about networks, as loosely-coupled structures that occupy the space between individual settings and broader systems? What is the potential of more strongly developed school networks?

- Does the sheer variety of promising schools and social contexts rule out uniform definitions of what should be expected of teachers? Or instead, are there "constants" of what the teacher is or should be? If learning is becoming more individualised and dependent on diverse sources, does this increase the demands on, and skills expected of, teachers? Or, do the same factors mean that the teacher is an increasingly redundant professional?

- What has been the influence of the established education authorities in individual cases – supportive or suspicious? Promoting or inhibiting? Do alternative schools offer a way for the future and can they do this without losing their "alternative" character? To what extent do the cases of innovatory schools form part of a programme of national policy in each country, or of particular policy initiatives? Are there tensions between national reforms and innovatory change at the institutional level?

The last question listed concerns the relationships between the micro and macro endeavours of change. And, in seeking to strike the balance between national reform policy and local innovation, there are the questions raised about what the appropriate roles are for governments, not just in terms of enacting reform but in supporting and sustaining innovation. What national initiatives are needed that find the balance: neither stifling the spirit of local initiative and teacher "ownership" of change nor risking that weaker schools never change? How best can governments create the conditions that support and spread innovation in schools, and is there a direct role in generalising innovation that "works"? What is the role in this of research, evaluation and dissemination? How can critical balances be struck: implementing national reforms that seek to ensure that all students and schools meet demanding learning aims without elaborating accountability mechanisms that defeat the very aims they are intended to ensure? How not to stymie genuine experimentation through excessive "top down" pressure? These are among the broader policy questions to be addressed beyond the lessons and practices of particular innovations.

Finally, alongside we should ask about the very future of the school itself. Will the answers to the above questions in years to come lead to modification of arrangements but no fundamental institutional change? Or instead should we imagine quite different arrangements where the school as such ceases to be recognisable or is no longer the learning venue for many young people? While we cannot expect to provide precise answers to such broad and unpredictable questions, we should continue the intense scrutiny of "the place called school".

Part I

HISTORICAL LESSONS AND FUTURE PERSPECTIVES

In this part, the experts look forward and back in understanding schooling for tomorrow, drawing on experiences in very different systems and world regions.

Kerry J. Kennedy, of the University of Canberra, Australia, examines curriculum issues against the background of growing social fragmentation and the "borderless world". With perhaps surprising unanimity, governments across very different systems agree about the importance of the curriculum and much of what it should comprise. Yet, without change, the author is not encouraged that many existing programmes will be up to the challenges of the next century. He advocates a shift from control to leadership in curriculum policies and places particular stress on developing non-cognitive ends – moral education, citizenship, a sense of community.

Walo Hutmacher, of the University of Geneva, Switzerland, offers a counterbalance to the focus on change and the future – he reflects on the constancy of what schools do. This is to address in particular their latent, as opposed to manifest, functions, which in turn requires a long-term, historical view. Identifying constancy is not to suppose that schools never change, and indeed sometimes they do in order to maintain continuity of purpose in changing circumstances. If there were new arrangements for the learning and socialisation of the young in the 21st century as a replacement for schools as we know them, such arrangements would need to fulfil a diversity of complex social, cultural and economic roles at least as well as this much-criticised but highly resilient institution.

Chapter 1

Constructing the School Curriculum for the Global Society

by

Kerry J. Kennedy
University of Canberra, Australia

Introduction

Traditionally, the main task of curriculum development has been to make decisions about which knowledge and skills should be included in the school curriculum. In some cases, such decisions are made at the school level by teachers and in
others they are made in centralised government agencies. Wherever the location of
the decision, the main point to note is that someone else makes decisions on
behalf of students. In doing so, a decision is also made not only to include certain
knowledge and skills but also to exclude others. In this sense, the school curriculum
is a bounded construct: serving specific needs and interests that may be personal,
social, political or economic. The school curriculum throughout the 20th century, the
age of mass education, has thus been limited and directed in its purposes.

Green (1997) has pointed to one reason for this in relation to the needs of the
developing nation state. Using case studies from Europe and Asia, he has shown
that as nations start to industrialise, they place considerable reliance on education
systems to deliver the knowledge and skills base needed for development. In addition, he has demonstrated that development and citizenship education also go
hand in hand as the State seeks to build its legitimacy over successive generations.
To achieve these purposes, there must be considerable control over the form and
content of the school curriculum.

Goodson and Marsh (1997) reinforce Green's views in their recent work on the
history of the school curriculum that takes into account historical developments in
North America, the United Kingdom and Australia. They show how competing interests have struggled to influence the curriculum towards ends and purposes that
suit themselves. At different times, different groups have been in the ascendancy
and the curriculum has been shaped to suit the views of those who have been able

to assert power. In this sense, the school curriculum has been constructed by the outcome of power relationships within the broader society.

A major issue for the 21st century is whether the degree of control that has been exercised over the school curriculum throughout the 20th century will be able to continue. Restricting access to knowledge, or at least to information, is becoming increasingly difficult. Already, information technology and communications have made it possible for young people to have access to knowledge on a scale unheard of just a decade ago. This trend is likely to increase as the 21st century approaches. If the school curriculum continues to be controlled either by governments or interests within society, the gap between "official" school knowledge and the real-world knowledge to which students can have access through information technology will widen. It may widen to the point where schools as they are known today may become irrelevant. This may mean that students will come to rely increasingly on sources of knowledge from outside schools. It may mean that more and more parents opt for home schooling where students will be able to develop for themselves a curriculum that suits their needs and interests and those of their parents. Such fragmentation would have a fundamental impact on society and the way individuals see themselves relating to each other.

The question for the 21st century, therefore, is how might the school curriculum create a sense of community and common values in a context where knowledge cannot be restricted in any way and where individual control is much more powerful than that which might be exerted by an external agency? Is there a role for the school curriculum in a world where there are no boundaries?

This chapter will explore two main areas in addressing this question:

– The current status of the school curriculum in the modern nation state with an emphasis on its controlling function and its uniformity across countries.

– The operation of the school curriculum in a world increasingly without borders.

The school curriculum in the modern nation state

In a study conducted by Kennedy and Mills (1996), curriculum policies in five Asia-Pacific states were reviewed in order to identify commonalities across the region as well as those unique features that characterise individual countries. The study was exploratory but yielded some outcomes relevant to the questions being addressed here.[1]

What are the similarities and differences between the areas of curriculum knowledge selected in each of the countries?

The most obvious set of comparisons to emerge was at the level of school subjects or areas of curriculum knowledge in each of the countries under review. Table 1 is an attempt to show similarities and differences across the five countries.

Table 1. **Areas of knowledge in the school curriculum of selected Asian Pacific countries**

PRC[1]	Hong Kong (China)[2]	United States[3]	Australia[4]	New Zealand[5]
Core = 85%	Core = 95%		Core = 100%	
Chinese	Chinese	English	English	English
Mathematics	Mathematics	Mathematics	Mathematics	Mathematics
Science	Science	Science	Science	Science and environment
Social subjects	History/geography/ Chinese history/ economics and public affairs	History/geography/ social studies	Studies of society and the environment	Social sciences
Physical education and health	Physical education	Physical education and health	Physical education and health	Physical and personal development
Arts	Arts/music	Arts	Arts	Arts
Foreign language	English Putonghua	Foreign language	LOTE	
Politics and moral education		Civics		
Labouring techniques				
	Computer literacy/ home economics/ design and technology		Technology	Technology

Sources: 1. Lai (1995).
2. Morris (1996).
3. Mills (1995).
4. Kennedy (1993).
5. Peddie (1995).

A number of points can be made about the data. A study of the mother tongue, mathematics and science is common to all countries. A study of one or more social studies is common as is an emphasis on arts education and physical and health education. Languages other than mother tongue are mandated in China (PRC), Hong Kong (China), Australia and the United States but not in New Zealand. Second language instruction in a specific language is mandated only in Hong Kong (China). Technology education has emerged in New Zealand, Australia and Hong Kong (China). "Labouring techniques" is unique to the PRC.

The degree of commonality should not be surprising. Four of the five countries emerged or are emerging from a colonial experience that was influenced by English educational ideology and practice and the PRC is seeking to adapt its education system to the needs of a "socialist market economy" (Lai, 1995). The emphasis on foreign languages in all but New Zealand is of interest and the rationale is more likely to be trade and economics rather than cultural enhancement. New Zealand's lack of interest in this area is difficult to explain. The emergence of technology education in three of the countries also suggests a responsiveness to new areas of knowledge in those countries, a responsiveness apparently missing in the United States and PRC. The equation of political and moral education in the PRC with civics in the United States might not be strictly accurate but provides an important discussion point as does the absence of similar formal studies from the other three countries.

The data in Table 1 are somewhat limited in the sense that they do not overtly reveal philosophical stances. Nevertheless, it is possible to detect in the major subject groupings a preference for an academic-rationalist approach to subject selection. Only in the PRC is there anything resembling vocational education as part of the core – labouring techniques appear to be a deliberate attempt to provide other than academic experiences as part of the schooling process. There is an emphasis in all countries on social and cultural formation and in Table 1 this appears to be accomplished in at least four countries through fairly traditional subject selections. PRC is the exception here but only because the data are more limited than those from the other four countries. Additional data would be needed to see whether all students spend an equal amount of time across the subject areas or whether some form of tracking directs students to different areas.

In what way is the school curriculum subject to policy direction?

In the past decade, governments in each of the countries under review had initiated major policy initiatives relating to the reform of the school curriculum. In the PRC the Nine Year Compulsory Education Programme was initiated in 1987 and supplemented by the Outline for Reform and Development of Education in China promulgated in 1993:

> "On-going reform of the subject content to strengthen moral and political education (...), the diversification of the subject curriculum by offering electives for the major subjects at secondary level, as well as the adjustment of teaching hours to cope with the new man-hour system (...)." (Lai, 1995, p. 2)

Ten years ago in Australia, the government issued a major statement on the school curriculum (Dawkins, 1988), and there followed from that an intensive five-year programme that sought to develop national curriculum statements and profiles for the compulsory years of schooling (Kennedy, 1993). In the United States, both Republican and Democratic administrations have supported a major effort of curriculum reform under the umbrella Goals 2000 that has been given specific legislative mandates and funding (Mills, 1995). In 1991, the New Zealand government released the National Curriculum of New Zealand as a discussion paper and by 1993 the final version was released (Peddie, 1995, p. 146). In 1993, the Hong Kong (China) Curriculum Development Council issued four major policy papers on the school curriculum covering kindergarten, primary, secondary and the sixth form. For the first time, the expectations of the school curriculum were codified and formally set out for public consumption (Morris, 1996).

Government interest in the school curriculum is by no means a new phenomenon and is certainly not a unique feature of the countries that were reviewed. Yet, the timing seems to be important given that all countries have devoted such attention to the school curriculum in the past five years. In addition, in at least two countries, Australia and the United States, action for curriculum reform has been taken by governments that themselves do not have constitutional responsibility for education. In both countries, such responsibility is with sub-national units such as State and Territory, rather than the central governments. Thus there appears to have been a national imperative for focusing on the school curriculum at this particular time.

Why have governments in the Asia-Pacific region, irrespective of their ideological complexion, taken such an interest in the school curriculum?

In at least four of the countries (United States, Australia, New Zealand and PRC), there has been an open embrace of human capital theory as a means of developing a more competitive economy capable of competing in the global arena. In Hong Kong (China), there is a more subtle blending of human capital theory and academic rationalism in the tracking of students by ability into academic and less academic curriculum areas. In all cases, the school curriculum is seen as an important means for providing students with knowledge and skills that will equip them to add some value to the economy.

Again, human capital theory is not a new influence on the curriculum. Informally, it has influenced economists at least since Adam Smith and more formally was codified in the 1960s to become a major influence on neo-classical economics. That it should emerge in the countries of the Asia-Pacific region at this time is itself an indication of the importance of economics to the region and especially to its governments.

While human capital theory seems to be a dominant influence, it is not the only one. In the United States, Australia, New Zealand and Hong Kong (China), there has also been the influence of "high standards" and "excellence". These concerns are not necessarily distinct from those of human capital theory since they can be related to the need to ensure high levels of achievement in areas that are crucial to economic development. At the same time, such concerns can also be related to the disaffection that many governments have with the schooling process, especially where educational innovation seems to sidetrack schools away from traditional academic concerns. "High standards in the curriculum" may well be a code for a traditional academic emphasis that governments, and the community in general, are able to endorse.

23

The review of the Kennedy and Mills (1996) findings here has demonstrated how the school curriculum towards the end of the 20th century is still seen very much as an instrument to secure the ends of the modern state. What is more, there is a remarkably similar approach to the curriculum taken by different nation states. There is uniformity rather than diversity in curriculum provision.

A major issue confronting policy-makers is whether schools can be maintained in this way in the light of advances in information and communications technology. With students and their parents having greater access to knowledge through technology-based innovation increasingly located in the home, will schools remain relevant in the 21st century?

Constructing the school curriculum in a borderless world: from control to leadership

The problem that will confront policy-makers in the 21st century is double-edged. If they continue to try to control the school curriculum, it may well become irrelevant to a generation able to access knowledge in ways unthought of two decades ago. On the other hand, if policy-makers accept the potential irrelevance of the traditional, structured curriculum, they may be tempted to adopt a decentralised approach to curriculum development that does not really address the problem. Handing control of the curriculum over to local interests simply creates another kind of control that is well known in democratic pluralistic states. Local curriculum control will probably lead to exactly the same outcome as if the problem of centralised control had not been recognised. The real issue for the 21st century is how to prevent fragmentation of the curriculum, whether that fragmentation results from central or local control.

To avoid fragmentation there is a need to move from a control mentality to a leadership mentality – from mandating details to setting directions. There are four broad areas in which action could be taken:

– To examine the theoretical impetus underlying the school curriculum.

– To define key competences for all students.

– To highlight the role of citizenship education.

– To focus on ethical behaviour and moral education.

Theoretical issues: from single to multiple conceptions of the school curriculum

Academic conceptions of the curriculum both help and hinder clarification of the issues under discussions. They help in the sense that they provide labels for the different conceptions that are articulated in the broader society. They hinder inasmuch as these labels tend to compartmentalise. Thus, when different orientations to curriculum are labelled as "academic", "instrumental", "self-actualisation", "social reconstructionist" or "critical", they construct barriers that suggest these

Figure 1. **Multiple perspectives on the school curriculum**

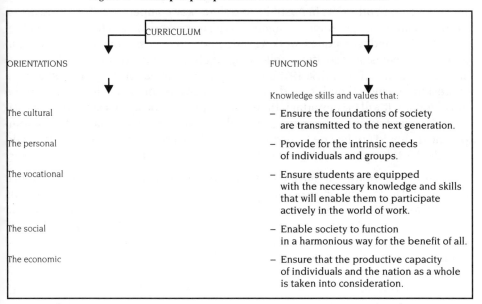

CURRICULUM

ORIENTATIONS

FUNCTIONS

Knowledge skills and values that:

The cultural
– Ensure the foundations of society
are transmitted to the next generation.

The personal
– Provide for the intrinsic needs
of individuals and groups.

The vocational
– Ensure students are equipped
with the necessary knowledge and skills
that will enable them to participate
actively in the world of work.

The social
– Enable society to function
in a harmonious way for the benefit of all.

The economic
– Ensure that the productive capacity
of individuals and the nation as a whole
is taken into consideration.

Source: Author.

orientations to be self-contained. The way ahead is not to construct barriers but to create new categories of thinking about the curriculum – categories that will be inclusive of the needs of all individuals and groups. This would create a model for the curriculum that would take into account the factors shown in Figure 1.

The main point to note about this proposed model is that the orientations and functions are not seen as mutually exclusive but as complementary, and all relevant in constructing the school curriculum. It is not a case of one or the other but of ensuring that the curriculum is able to meet the needs of all individuals and groups.

Defining key competences for all students

Given that the school curriculum will be characterised by diversity rather than uniformity in the 21st century, will there be a need to define skills and competences that all students ought to have irrespective of their specific curriculum experience? The question is a modernist one, it is also important. Access to knowledge and skills will as much provide access to well-being and power in the future as it does now. Unless society in the future is to be determined entirely by the law of the market, there will remain a need to guarantee a minimum level of knowledge and skills for all future citizens.

25

Defining what is essential in a fragmenting world is not an easy task. Recently, there have been attempts in Australia to define "key competences". In some areas, there is significant agreement: communicating ideas and information; using mathematical ideas and techniques; working with others in teams; using technology; planning and organising activities; collecting, analysing and organising information; solving problems (Borthwick, 1993). Yet in others, there has also been considerable contestation: cultural understanding and life management skills have evoked the most debate. It will be important, therefore, to build a consensus around what society values and what can be made part of the experience of all students. Key competences should not just be focused on the world of paid employment; they should include the full range of skills and competences relevant throughout the life span.

It is also important to have a clear view about competences and competence in general. There is one view of competence that focuses on behaviouristic notions of performance and attempts to build competence from discrete bits of behaviour. This is now outmoded. More recent work (Gonczi *et al.*, 1990; Heywood *et al.*, 1992; Hager, 1994; Walker, 1993; Preston and Walker, 1994) suggests that competence is a matter of integrating knowledge, skills and values in such a way that competent performance results. Performance itself is not competence, as it is in the older behaviouristic notions. Rather, performance is an indicator that the competence is held. Competence can be inferred; it cannot be observed. Thus tasks provide the opportunity for students to demonstrate competence and when this occurs it can be assumed that the student has brought together and understood the relationship between a range of knowledge, skills and values. This makes the issue of assessment crucial as well as complex, while it also enriches the understanding of competence (Hager and Butler, 1994; Preston and Kennedy, 1995).

A key requirement is to generate a debate about what is central for young people in the 21st century and to make the outcome of such debate the centre-piece of the curriculum. The debate should not become overly concerned with specific content. Instead, it should concentrate on the skills and competences that transcend content. This is not to dismiss the cultural significance of content; that, too, is an important debate. Rather, the focus needs to be on those processes that will enable young people to access knowledge, to understand, critique, and transform it, and to do so on a lifelong basis. This is the imperative for the next century.

Highlighting the role of citizenship education

How will citizenship be constructed in the 21st century? In the past, formal courses in civics education have concentrated on the structures of government and on constructing an historical context into which all citizens are meant to fit. This will not do for the 21st century. It will be important to develop a civics education that takes into account present-day realities and future needs. Of key importance is the idea that what is reality for adults is not necessarily so for young people.

Whether it is techno music, rave parties, drug-taking or early experimentation with sex, young people come under great pressure to conform to peer expectations and emerging fads. Much of the pressure comes from peers, but there are also the mass media sending constant messages about what is new and desirable. Civics education cannot neglect these realities of life for young people, even though they may not be realities for those designing civics education programmes. Often such issues are seen as part of a broader youth culture although it is probably true that there is no longer a single discernible trend in youth culture but many trends depending on which young people, with which priorities, in which locations, are in question. Young people cannot be left to cope with issues such as personal identity in the hope of constructing some national identity for them all. Civics education, broadly conceived, could act as a bridge between personal and national identities, so that young people are able to develop a sense of themselves and how they relate to their peers and others with whom they share the planet.

The influence of youth culture on young people is but one social condition that confronts them. Post-school options are now very limited with further education and training offering the best chance for future employment. The spectre of unemployment looms large for many young people. It adds to the uncertainty that is part of the lives of so many. This uncertainty is not helped by the experience of many in the casual labour market where they often put up with poor working conditions, low wages and arbitrary management practices. There is little that any educational programme can do about this social context. Yet, it is important to understand and take account of it in any purpose-designed civics education programme. The ancient Greeks realised only too well that citizens needed to benefit from citizenship if they were to be called on to participate actively in the life of the *polis*. It may be difficult to convince young people today of the benefits that accrue to them from their citizenship in a society that is unable to guarantee them access to the rewards that others seem to have in such abundance.

Yet, democratic citizenship is not only about benefits, it is also about responsibilities. There is now a significant literature on the role of service learning in civics education. Basically, this means providing young people with the opportunity to contribute to their communities by becoming involved in worthwhile activities. Thus, civics education should take students outside the classroom so that they can learn some of the responsibilities of citizenship. They can link up with community service organisations that assist the elderly, are concerned with environmental issues or that support disaffected youth. Young people can serve their communities and in this way come to understand better the responsibilities of citizenship.

Students do not, of course, have to leave their classrooms to experience working in a democracy. The classroom itself, and indeed the whole school community, offers opportunities for democratic living. Whether this is done through student representative councils, mock parliaments or representation on school committees, _27_ students can have direct first-hand experience of what living in a democracy is like. They can experience the joys and the frustrations of democratic participation. Democracy should not be understood solely as something that was developed in the past or occurs through periodic elections; it should be about lived experience in a multitude of contexts.

Citizens of the future will be international citizens. They will require a knowledge base that will help them feel as comfortable in other countries as they do in their own. Regional groupings such as APEC, NAFTA and EU indicate that national boundaries are becoming irrelevant as nations seek advantages from cross-national activities and enterprises. Common reference to "European citizenship", for example, highlights how far at least one region of the world has come just fifty years after a devastating war. There will always be local citizenship, but in the future it will be exercised in a different context: global communication and international travel will mean that it will be difficult to know when borders have been crossed. Young people need to be prepared for such a future so that the international and the national can co-exist and feed off one another. There is surely a role for civics education here if young people are to be prepared for such a future.

Focusing on ethical behaviour and moral education

In an increasingly fragmented world, what is to be made of ethics and morality? If the question again seems to be that of the modernist, there is still a need for young people to be confronted with what is meant by ethical behaviour and why it is important. The reason is not to indoctrinate, but to arm young people. They need to be able to distinguish right and wrong, recognise it in the behaviour of others, and to take appropriate action.

History is littered with examples of whole societies being unable to discern right from wrong and embarking on practices that have been contrary to the human spirit and soul. This century alone has witnessed death camps, gulags, torture, discrimination, persecution and wars on an international scale. Nuclear weapons, chemical warfare and smart bombs have demonstrated extraordinary skill and knowledge but at the same time revealed a world that needs to understand and value the people who live in it. Technological innovation and values have not always gone together.

At the same time, experience has also shown that attempts to impose a single set of values on a disparate society rarely succeed. Indeed, such attempts often lead to regimes that defeat the very purpose of establishing a set of values in the first place. Enforcement of common values can be a painful process that results in confusing means and ends and that reifies the process of enforcement rather than the values that are intended to be defended. Common values underpinned by a compliance regime are not the way ahead for the 21st century.

The 21st century citizen must learn those values that respect the human spirit, and its hopes, dreams and aspirations. Those citizens will have different ideas about those dreams and they will have different ways of working towards them. They may or may not share a view about the ultimate purposes for living; they may indeed hold quite opposite views. But they should recognise this difference as positive; ideally, they will celebrate the difference. What can bring all citizens together is this respect for difference and an ability to see how difference means a richer, more varied and diverse experience for everyone. Difference can be shared and therefore appreciated. It should not be what divides citizens, but what brings them together in an effort to learn more from, and about, one another.

How to bring about this kind of moral or ethical education will be one of the most significant challenges facing us in the 21st century. It must be on the educational agenda if societies are not to disintegrate or break down because the only principle operating is that of self-interest. Young citizens must first be taught to value values. They will need to be people who have a thought-out set of values for themselves and who respect other people's values. They will at times see virtue in sacrificing personal gain for the good of others, and accept that the common good will not always meet their own personal needs. Balancing the personal and the common will be the moral dilemma facing many young people in the 21st century.

The sources of morality and ethics will be as contested in the next century as they have been over time. Different nations, and groups within nations, have looked to religion of one kind or another for their inspiration. That search will undoubtedly continue. Others have looked to secular issues such as environmental protection, the elimination of discriminatory practices against different groups, and the protection of children from exploitation. These areas provide a source not only of values but of explicit social action designed to restore harmony in fractured relationships. Thus, the difference between overtly religious and secular values has been blurred. In Australia, for example, the strongest voice in support of reconciliation with indigenous peoples has been the churches. In the future, the barriers that exist between the secular and religious may be broken down so that all who embrace positive values can come together. This would certainly provide a platform to assist young people to value values as a central part of the life experience.

A sense of community in a fragmenting world?

A further fundamental question facing policy-makers in the 21st century will be how to provide leadership that will facilitate social cohesion in an otherwise fragmented world. One approach would be that described by Gale (1994) in relation to education policy in general. He referred to the notion of "education policy settlements" that masquerade as solutions to policy problems. The settlements are usually short term in nature and there is often a need for resettlements when the problem surfaces again.[2] The concept of "settlement" is a useful one in underlining that solutions can be found, that they will involve negotiation, and that they might well contain what appear to be ideologically inconsistent constituents.

What will be needed in the 21st century will be curriculum settlements that allow communities to come together and agree about the directions the school curriculum will take. No one should be excluded from these deliberations, and particularly not the students. Directives from head office, or even the principal's office, will not work. If there is to be a commitment to a common citizenship, and a common set of skills and values, then citizens will need to be involved in determining these. This will be the *sine qua non* of the 21st century. As barriers and structures are removed in all areas of activity, citizens will become used to making decisions for themselves. It will be no different in education. Participative, collaborative mechanisms must lay the foundation for curriculum in the 21st century. An urgent task of governments and policy-makers is to put such mechanisms into place so that the new millennium can be informed by a curriculum process and outcomes that meet the real need for community in an otherwise fragmenting world. To ignore this task will be to risk the futures of the young people of the 21st century.

Chapter 2

Invariants and Change in Schools and Education Systems

by

Walo Hutmacher
University of Geneva, Switzerland

The focus on the invariants of education

"Schooling for tomorrow" is a rich theme that invites endless speculation, discussion and projection. The natural focus is on *change*; the underlying assumption is that the school of tomorrow will or should be different from today's school and very different from yesterday's. At the start of the CERI reflection on this important subject, however, I would like to focus less on change and more on the *constants* or *invariants*. For, while the profound transformations of recent decades give the impression that everything has changed and may lead us to believe that tomorrow's schools will be very different from today's, a preoccupation with change prevents a rounded analysis. The assessment of what remains constant must also be entered into the account, and this in a number of ways.

First, there is virtually no change without constants. Certain dimensions of schools and education systems have remained stable despite the significant changes of the last decades. Identifying these constants can help us to identify those aspects of schooling that otherwise constitute so many blind spots in our perception of today's reality and of our projections about tomorrow. Indeed, overlooking these points of stability can block the changes we believe are desirable because we are then operating with only a partial analysis of the situation relating to schools. Conversely, focusing on schools' constants can help to identify those aspects of education systems and schools that must continue to remain constant so the changes we seek can take effect.

Second, there is the need to distinguish fundamental from superficial change. Some changes preserve the prevailing order of things and relations under changing conditions; in this sense, they represent constancy. Higher-level changes are more fundamental, however, because they modify that prevailing order. Watzlawick *et al.* (1988) have shown very well how much the relation between what changes and what does not determines whether a change is fundamental or not. Addressing constants may therefore enable us to understand how fundamental are the changes that we perceive, anticipate or seek to foster.

Furthermore, looking for constants in a changing field forces us to consider the reality of the education system and its schools rather than the normative ideals or critiques, which abound in discussions concerning schooling for tomorrow. Rather than simply elaborating normative propositions about schools as we would like to see them, such a focus can help identify constraints in the system that should not be ignored in the enthusiasm to formulate desirable futures.

Yet, despite the value of identifying invariants in education, they are more difficult to grasp than change or innovation. Change, be it political or pedagogical, is made visible in public discourse and debate. It may be praised or condemned, but it enjoys a social existence. Constants, on the other hand, are far less in the public eye, partly because they belong to what is self-evident and familiar. At least two approaches can be pursued.

One approach is to develop an understanding through the *history of education*. This can be highly revealing of the decisions and arguments that have, over time, forged the specific social arrangements we now call "schools" and "education systems". History provides the means to document and better understand the development of our institutions, the result of long, often conflictual processes of social and political construction of representations, beliefs, and practices. It also brings to light the debates concerning definitions of "youth", "family", "education" and "schools" that have been progressively forgotten as these major social constructions, that are now at the heart of education, have become institutionalised. They are so familiar as to appear bound to continue as the parameters of education. Yet, understanding such changes through an historical perspective can help to clarify how necessary the everyday features of our institutions actually are, or whether their rationale derives from an era when different conditions prevailed.

A second approach is to view schools and school systems as *multi-functional structures* with many effects at the individual and collective levels, only some of which are explicitly stated as objectives or goals. In general, schools have observable effects that extend well beyond the system's stated, explicit objectives. Such an approach starts by assuming that no observable effect need be regarded as abnormal or "dysfunctional" so long as it results from the system's regular operation; such regularly occuring effects that do not correspond to the system's explicit goals can be understood as latent rather than manifest functions. Observable effects may thus not correspond to the goals assigned to schools; they may even bear no relation to or contradict the explicit goals. But, insofar as these effects regularly result from schools' operations, they should be considered as regular functions – educational contributions to other systems or to society at large.

It is impossible to give a full analysis of all the explicit and latent functions of schools and education systems and the characteristics that have remained constant throughout the major movements of the last decades. It is possible, however, to identify some of these, and to lay the basis for reflection on the fuller picture.

Schools: constantly criticised – but they survive

Critical debate has existed since the creation of schools. They have been criticised since their emergence in Europe in the 16th century – for what they teach, how they operate, what they cost, what students learn and even more for what they do not learn. There has never been an extended period of consensus about the quality or the effectiveness of schools. But neither, despite such criticism, has there been a period when the very existence of schools as particular learning institutions has been seriously at issue. Proposals to abolish schools, like the one launched by Ivan Illich in the 1970s (Illich, 1971), have given rise to lively debate but they have not seriously taken root.

The school as a specific institutional arrangement is itself a constant. It has outlived many religious, political, social and economic crises and expanded in times of massive urbanisation and industrialisation. Over time, all modern nations have developed school systems. Hence, the school must enjoy a selective advantage of some kind over other possible models of education. Something about them "works", constant criticisms notwithstanding: whether schools, individually or collectively, work "well" or "badly" in terms of their own goals is another matter.

The point can be illustrated by everyday observation. In OECD countries, millions of students are assembled daily in hundreds of thousands of schools and classrooms. Some will qualify for a diploma, while others will leave school more or less early without acquiring the competence expected. These processes occur in a relatively disciplined, orderly fashion; even in schools with populations of several hundreds of children and young people, massive disruption is rare (though, of course, there are other manifestations of violence). It is interesting to reflect on the ways in which such multitudes are managed in a more or less disciplined fashion, and examine the differences that exist among schools in this respect. We might also ask about the cost of maintaining such order. Such reflection will most likely lead to the conclusion that there are aspects of what schools do that really "work". If they were totally dysfunctional, as some critics have supposed, they would not have survived for so long, still less to have expanded markedly over recent decades. People would not spend such large parts of their lives in them. States and tax-payers would not spend substantial sums on them.

Given, then, that they are functional, in some or many ways, we should ask precisely what it is they do contribute to society or at least to the interests of its dominant groups, whether explicitly or in more hidden, latent ways. How do they

_33_

work? What specific social contributions do they make to individual and collective players?

Educability and change

As an integral part of modernity, the school is rooted in two strong beliefs that distinguish our civilisation from most others in human history:

- That the world can be changed by educating, and hence changing, people; societal problems can be addressed through education, specifically through the work of schools and school systems.
- That the feasibility of society, of historically developed arrangements of institutions, relations, structure and culture, also means that it is possible to change schools.

The strong basis of belief in the educability of human beings and malleability of human nature, representing a long historical tradition, is a rarely-questioned premise nowadays when most debate focuses instead on the desirability of specific educational outcomes on the assumption of such educability. This premise has been seriously questioned only indirectly, in debates around correct and fair methods of education. For the last two decades, the social sciences have explored the conditions under which human beings learn but the conclusions remain uncertain and have yet had only marginal effects on defining how schools should be structured and run. Such research has not served to undermine the key assumption of educability.

Over time, the school as an institution has been accorded a wide range of social responsibilities: forging common religious beliefs, patriotic convictions, morals, and teaching literacy, numeracy, rational analysis and scientific knowledge. Recently, schools have been expected to address other social issues such as sex education and AIDS, traffic, tolerance, non-violence, employability, social cohesion, and the environment, among others. Thus, changing societies require that schools change, but the demand for schools itself remains constant.

The major invariant of education systems over time is the school itself. That we can come together from so many countries and traditions to talk about schools in international seminars like this one in Hiroshima demonstrates that we all include schools and school systems in our definitions of education. Looked at as a whole, national differences appear as variations around a shared institutional model, a common set of social representations and practices we refer to as "school".

The structure of educational authority

This educational model is grounded in a specific combination of educational authority, rights and obligations distributed between families and other private educators, on the one hand, and the school or education system, as a collective,

34

publicly controlled institution, on the other. Historically, the school represents a form of public appropriation of children and their education from parents and families. Most countries have declared some form of instruction compulsory at one point or another, a clear expression of the will of religious and then political authorities to exercise control over the education of the population.

Geneva's citizens, for example, are proud to have been among the first political communities to declare schooling compulsory in the 16th century. The same assembly of citizens that decided the foundation of the Protestant Republic of Geneva in 1536 also declared that this republic "will fund a school [...] *and oblige all parents* to have their children attend it". Public rule over education was strongly reaffirmed in the constituent parliament during the French Revolution: "youth belongs to society and thus to the State". The same, longstanding argument was repeated in different guises during the 19th century when modern European states were being formed. In most countries, as in Geneva, the legal obligation only became really effective during the 19th century when schooling was broadly accepted even by the urban working class and rural communities, and the modern state could afford the economic burden of universal schooling and the enforcement of compulsory attendance using police and the courts.

The structural tension inherent in the distribution of educational responsibilities between parents and families, on one side, and schools, on the other, constitutes another constant. Families, and parents in particular, are primarily responsible for long-term emotional ties and have legal, moral and economic responsibility for their children's personal and social destiny. At the same time, schools have the right to influence what children and youngsters learn and come to believe, sometimes despite parents' wishes. They play a major role in assessing and judging the competences that strongly shape students' career prospects. While parents have lifelong moral and economic responsibility for their children, school responsibility extends over a shorter period. With this historical asymmetrical division of educational responsibility and authority, schools and education systems have been regulated by political bodies rather than by the market, even in the most liberal and capitalistic countries.

Tensions are nevertheless in evidence. Lately, the increasing influence of parents' associations, and growing number of court trials over school matters suggest that the legitimacy of these unequal rights and obligations is being called into question, especially by a well-educated middle class. While education remains one of the most accepted of state responsibilities, tensions are developing around the degree and type of control it should exercise. What state level should control which levels of the education system? How much autonomy should be left to the schools and their professionals, and in which areas? Questions have arisen about the nature of the state's prerogative: should it continue to extend to the direct operation of the schools and the delivery of what are now called educational services, and for what level or type of education?   35

Yet, whatever their degree of autonomy, schools and teachers are never entirely free to decide what, how, or whom they teach, and under what temporal, spatial or social conditions. Between the 15th and the 16th centuries, the authority for deciding educational goals and contents came to reside in structures outside the school itself, and this principle has since been well established. This external power is stronger in public education systems, but even private schools depend more or less directly on some external authority to define or control their objectives and the knowledge and behaviour they are to transmit. At the same time, this external authority also defines standards of excellence and the selection process through which students are admitted to particular schools or courses of study. Certain forms of knowledge and belief are thus selectively declared legitimate subjects for study while many aspects of everyday culture are not (*e.g.* slang, dialects). Students are selected for or barred from certain types of knowledge. What is included in a curriculum is always more visible than what is excluded. But, in the resolution of these matters, there are constant tensions.

Ultimately, an educational authority controls more or less closely the legitimate means of transmitting knowledge, beliefs and competences and the legitimate ways of exercising power and authority over students. Even when didactics, textbooks and teaching methods lie outside the external authority's sphere of responsibility, teacher training and selection conventionally lie within it. Indeed, while schools are supposed primarily to be about the students, most legal and regulatory prescriptions focus on the activity of the adults (teachers and other professionals), in terms of prescribing legitimate activities.

The constants of schools as formal organisations

Schools can be looked at as formal organisations: they have arrangements of roles, places and positions, within a specific power structure and division of labour, that give them closure. Those who criticise this organisational closure often miss the point that a school would simply not exist as a specialised organisation without the differentiation of its physical and social space from everyday activities of normal adult life. In most cases, parents do not belong to the organisation and their role is considered external to the school itself. Certain of these organisational features warrant closer attention.

Selection, assignment, assessment

Students are assigned to classes and levels by age and by previous achievements; they are taught and controlled by teachers whom they do not choose and who do not choose them. Teachers depend on principals, and sometimes inspectors, in most cases choosing neither. Responsibilities are individualised, in the sense that teachers and students are held responsible only for their own behaviour and achievements. Typically, students are organised in classes rather than teams.

Even when teachers teach the same group of students in succeeding grades, they remain individuals responsible for a limited time and/or subject matter, and team-teaching is not the norm. Overall responsibility for the whole pathway of students through the school is only loosely structured, at best.

Student assessment and assignment to levels or streams tends to be highly formalised and impersonal, as is progress through the school. As a simple example, a young mother with a daughter who was to enter the first grade of primary school which is dedicated to learning to read, told me how she had informed the teacher that her daughter had already mastered the basics. The teacher declared, "I will make no distinction between her and the rest, learning to read is on the programme of the first grade, that's all there is to it." Cases like this one are not universal, but such a position is regarded as a legitimate attitude in normal schools: as a formal organisation, the school operates with categories rather than with persons.

School objectives

Formally, schools are governed through defined objectives that are for the most part formulated in rather vague terms, leaving much to interpretation. In reality, achievements and behaviour are evaluated less in terms of their conformity with these objectives than with prescribed rules and norms. Teacher assessment where it occurs, for instance, tends to be based more on teaching a prescribed curriculum, or on regularity, punctuality and the capacity to maintain discipline, than on the learning outcomes from that teaching. There is a strong trend towards what, in sociological terminology, might be called bureaucratic regulation in contrast with professional regulation.

The social game induced by these features has many effects on student learning. Students certainly learn to cope with rules and norms that define tasks and civilities about which they have little say; these rules and norms are impersonal in that they are universal, and apply to individuals defined as roles rather than persons. The process of learning to live and work within a formal, hierarchical, bureaucratically-regulated organisation is not part of a school's explicit objectives, but is clearly an important part of schools' contribution to ensuring that students can function well in a future workplace. This may indeed be considered as one of the most important latent school functions. Were the nature of organisations outside schools, especially workplaces, to change significantly, however, one might then expect pressures to mount for schools to change in this regard as well.

Temporal and spatial arrangements

Schools typically operate with a very formalised calendar: the great majority of them on the basis of a curriculum to be taught and learned additively in a given number of years, sub-divided into smaller periods of working months, weeks and days. Each day is divided into a number of lessons lasting some 40-50 minutes. The fact that this very typical time arrangement forces students to "zap" every 45 or 90 minutes from one subject to another is generally considered a necessary evil. Closer examination, however, reveals how much this apparently disjointed time structure is connected with the bureaucratic allocation of students' time to different teachers. There is little basis for this arrangement from the point of view of efficient learning, but while it might be frequently criticised, it continues to characterise a typical school day.

Schools also have typical spatial arrangements, characterised by closure to the outside. Internally, their buildings are segmented into classrooms of more or less standard size with standard equipment. Since school buildings change significantly only very occasionally, the physical structures affect several generations of students and teachers and represent a strong element of inertia. They operate over the long haul to constrain the modification of relationships within schools.

The constancy of schools' latent functions

Schools and school systems are by nature multi-functional and have many effects on individuals and groups. Some of their functions correspond to explicit goals and expectations, defined by laws and regulations or in prescribed curricula. These goals are very often formulated in terms of individual development and learning related to certain areas of competence, knowledge and attitude. In most countries, schools and school systems have long had primary responsibility for assessing student achievement. Today, the situation is changing through assessment becoming increasingly external to the school, as seen in the development of national and international comparative surveys on outcomes.

The level and the extent to which student populations learn and master requisite competences is becoming a more explicit criterion for judging educational quality, and emphasises this key manifest contribution that schools make. We should come back, however, to the observable implicit contributions of education – the latent functions. An historical perspective is useful again. In the 16th century, for instance, the school providing a common experience for a young generation of the *élite* was considered to strengthen that elite's cultural and social integration, in a fashion that could not be achieved with the prevailing arrangement of private preceptor instruction in families. While not a specified goal, there was a clear expectation of an effect on social and cultural integration, an effect which has if anything increased in importance in more recent highly pluralistic and segmented modern societies. Cementing social cohesion continues to be one of the school's major contributions. In the 19th century, a clear benefit of compulsory elementary schools was perceived to be that it kept children out of the streets and factories. This custodial function is also becoming even more important today given growing numbers of families with two working parents. Yet, this effect is not explicitly included among the major objectives of schools, and it is often resented by teachers.

One of the most important latent school and school system functions is in legitimising the differentiation of social status in each new generation and the distribution of individuals among unequal working positions. This function never appears in the formal definition of goals but is as old as schools themselves. Erasmus of Rotterdam's De Civilitate morum puerilium ("Children's' civility") was published in 1531 and used in schools long thereafter throughout Europe. The author considered that this collection of precepts for civil behaviour dealt with the "most humble part of philosophy", but nevertheless claimed an equivalence, in its preface, between "those who cultivate their spirit through the practice of the humanities" and the accepted nobility by birth. This distinguished commoner was expressing more than his own aspirations for elevation. His claim was that the bourgeoisie could be distinguished from (more) ordinary people and acquire a new kind of "nobility" through learning. From the 16th until at least the end of the 19th century in Europe, schools have been the main vehicles of this bourgeois aspiration. Colleges, while mainly promoted and run by the Church, were consistently founded with the political and financial support of the bourgeoisie, primarily for its own children. Schools thus offered access to the standards of excellence and the legitimacy of a higher social standing, at that time through mastery of the classical humanities.

Today's standards of social excellence are different. Moreover, education systems encompass much more than elites and, since the 19th century, have a more clearly utilitarian orientation towards preparing students to work. Under the Ancien Régime, the process of social distinction was partly external to schools since only the upper classes had access to them. Modern schools and education systems, as they cover the whole population, have internalised the process of re-distributing unequal social value and status. Yet, individuals' prospects more than ever depend on academic qualification and its formal recognition in the form of the diploma. The school is thus critical in a person's position upon entering the labour market, which can itself prove largely determinant of subsequent social standing. In recent years, qualifications can even determine whether a student will enter the labour market at all. After entry, job assessments regularly consider formally recognised education requirements for a job, and diplomas are considered a legitimate basis for determining salaries. All the relevant indicators, including OECD figures, demonstrate that education correlates highly with earnings and life-chances. Even if this correlation is only an association in terms of probabilities not certainties, the differences are very significant.

The role of assessment here is critical. It is an aspect of normal school operations which consumes much time and energy. But while explicitly formulated goals tend to be framed in terms of students' learning and achievements per se, schools' roles in actually conducting assessments tend to be taken for granted. This is despite the importance of student assessment for everyday and long-term experience and the key role of evaluation as a driving activity of students, teachers and schools. Many students work in relation to assessment regimes, and are clever enough to pace their work investment and direct their studies to keep their grades above average. Working to tests and grades reflects a good understanding of bureaucratic regulation. Again, there is an important distance between the explicit goals of school systems framed in terms of learning and what actually takes place.

The assessments that take place in schools result in differentiation and certification: the qualifications of some students are acknowledged while disqualifying others. This selection process has an objective, social dimension, and a subjective, individual one. Objectively, schools' judgements contribute to determining a student's social standing and reward, in the eyes of fellow students, parents, friends, future teachers, and employers. Subjectively, qualified students accept the validity of such judgements, tending to attribute their achievements to personal merit. After repeated reinforcements, the most disqualified students rarely protest nor blame the school but make its judgement their own, attributing their "failure" to personal inability. This is consistent with the theory of attribution and locus of control. For both qualified and disqualified students, assessment underpins not only grades and diplomas but also self-image, and this is consistently reinforced by its effect on social reputation. Over time, students who qualify consider themselves able and worthy, while the reverse holds for those who do not qualify who voluntarily temper their social aspirations accordingly.

Given the profound impacts of school assessments, it is valuable to consider that schools consistently assess more than they have actually taught (see Perrenoud, 1984). Many of the attitudes, and some of the knowledge and skills rewarded in school are learned, mainly or in part, outside school. How well this external learning leads to successful schooling strongly depends on family background and socio-economic status. Comparative formal assessments and recognition in schools barely take into account students' unequal family contexts and preparation, even though the potency of these extra-school influences is well-known.

Thus, we can identify another key constant of schools and education systems, the importance of which is not diminished by its familiarity: children who achieve least well in schools, with all the social and economic consequences that follow from that, come disproportionately from culturally and economically poor backgrounds. The education system contributes powerfully to the process of legitimation of the unequal re-distribution of desirable social destinies. This is one of its major contributions to the relatively peaceful operation of democratic but unequal societies. If the school system did not perform this function, what other social institution would be in a position to do so, and in such a subtle manner? The subtlety is indeed noteworthy: the school simultaneously organises the process of qualification and disqualification, operates at both objective and subjective levels, and this over a sufficiently long period during childhood and youth as to be effective for a lifetime. This is reinforced as the well-educated are much more likely to enjoy continued access to education and become lifelong learners.

Noting these effects is not intended as an exercise in conspiracy theory. While the conclusions so derived might be uncomfortable for many, I have sought to take a realistic approach to a complex social reality. It is anyway not a conspiracy as the process is unplanned, even unanticipated. That is just how it is – schools and education systems reproduce and legitimize social inequality. The significance of this function, particularly for the leading groups and classes in modern societies, is one of the major reasons for the prominence of educational debates and the continuing existence of schools despite persistent criticism, as discussed at the beginning. It must be recognised, however, that there is plenty of scope for conflict and incompatibility between this latent, selective function and generous goals such as "high quality education for all" espoused at high level events like OECD education ministerial conferences.

* * *

This brief presentation of some key structural and functional constants of schools and education systems is, of course, not exhaustive but it does seek to trace the main elements and to lay the basis for further analysis. There is an underlying methodological stance: to engage in serious reflection on the school of tomorrow must include precisely such constants, even when it is uncomfortable to do so because they seem to contradict the explicit aims of policy.

This form of analysis suggests the sorts of questions to be addressed in relation to different scenarios for change and specific innovations. What changes and what does not? Will schools continue to exist? For what and for whom? Who will control and run them? How will educational authority be distributed between school and families? What degree of autonomy will be given to individual schools and to professionals and in what areas? Will temporal and spatial arrangements and roles change? Will internal regulation remain as bureaucratic as it has become to date? Is there scope for a more professional regulation based on the attainment of goals? How will the school and education system manage the potential incompatibility between aiming for high competence for all and the fact and function of unequal social origins and destinations? Even more important is to ask: how will education systems and individual schools learn to deal realistically with themselves, with their change and their constants, while projecting themselves into the future?

OECD 1999

Part II

INNOVATION AND CHANGE

This part focuses on the importance of innovation in education, its characteristics and how the policy aim of supporting innovation lies in tension – sometimes creative, sometimes inhibiting – with other aims and characteristics of education systems.

David H. Hargreaves, of the University of Cambridge, United Kingdom, as Kennedy in Chapter 1, is not encouraged that the bureaucratic, "factory models" of schooling will survive well into the world of the 21st century. Too many schools in public systems can still be characterised as belonging to this mould, lacking flexibility and innovation. Increasingly, parents, the community, and the world of work demand more, which could well lead to the continued diversification of institutional forms of education to meet these demands. A priority for policy and practice is now to invest in educational innovation, which is not to be confused with introducing more "top-down" reform.

The nature and practice of innovation in education is the subject of the chapter by Francoise Cros, of the Institut national de recherche pédagogique (INRP), Paris, France. Attention to and support of school innovation has been growing, and the tensions between national reform and localised experiment and renewal are in a process of dynamic change. Nor are particular innovations themselves constant but subject to processes of normalisation and institutionalisation, if they survive at all. There are different traditions and metaphors through which innovation may be understood, as well as different actors involved. The role of the intermediary in particular warrants close analysis.

Chapter 3

Schools and the Future: the Key Role of Innovation

by

David H. Hargreaves
University of Cambridge, United Kingdom

Introduction

In recent times, governments throughout the world have been reforming school systems to enhance educational standards and thereby ensure that more young people reach ever higher levels of knowledge and skill in the fierce international competition for economic success. In many countries, there has been, within the reforms, a focus on "the basics" to ensure that all students in the primary phase achieve as quickly as possible the literacy and numeracy which provide essential access to the rest of the school curriculum. At secondary level and beyond, a main focus has been on better preparation of students for the world of work, which has raised questions about the nature, appropriateness and quality of pre-vocational and vocational education and how these relate both to the mainstream school curriculum and to the wider educational purposes of schooling.

These concerns, which are long-standing on the policy agenda, are now accompanied by some new themes, including how what is learned in school, not just the content of the curriculum but also motivation and commitment to learning, and prepares the young for lifelong learning and, as part of this, how skills in the use of the new information and communication technologies can be fostered in school. Both relate to "the basics", for computer literacy is now as fundamental as reading, and also to vocational education, as the world of work is itself increasingly permeated by the new information and communication technologies.

The changing world of work and employment

The structure of the world of work is changing very rapidly as traditional industrial society comes to an end and is replaced by the "knowledge society" which generates different types and patterns of work. It is one of the functions of schools to prepare the young, directly or indirectly, for working life; and certainly young people and their parents value schooling because of its potential relevance to later employment. So, changes in the nature of work in the next century are profoundly relevant to the functions and character of schools. The major fear is of increasing unemployment. In a recent British survey, 82 per cent of parents and 73 per cent of school students expressed concern about the lack of jobs for the young. The concern is understandable, since there are 18 million unemployed people in the European Union and many millions more who would like work. Even in countries where unemployment is – for the moment, at least – relatively low, the same questions are being asked:

– Will *full employment be restored*? One would like to hope so, but most observers are pessimistic. There will probably not be enough to provide all who want it with full-time paid employment.

– Will *paid employment largely disappear*? It is too early to say. If it does, then we shall have to develop a work ethic to replace the employment ethic. In other words, people will need to learn that there is worthwhile work to be done even though it may not have a salary or wage attached and it may not be done for an employer.

– Will *paid employment have to be shared or rationed in some way*? Almost certainly if we are to avoid a world in which a few relatively rich people take all the paid employment and the less well off majority have no jobs at all. It is often predicted that the future will bring a "de-jobbed", portfolio society: that is to say, one where for most people lifelong careers give way to a series of jobs and where most paid employment is part-time and/or non-permanent since work has to be rationed.

The changing character of schooling

The implications of such a world for the education system and for schools have yet to be clarified. Schools in their traditional form have been patterned on the factory system. For over 150 years, schools have effectively socialised the young to the world of employment in the industrial era by age-graded classes of children following lessons punctuated by bells. As the era passes, the schools will have to change. In any event, the pattern of schooling is already undergoing change because of a range of factors.

Consider three of the educational sectors in the United Kingdom at the present time:

– the comprehensive school, or common secondary school;

– the specialist school;

– home schooling.

Of the three, the *comprehensive* school is the largest and by far the most important. By a *specialist* school, I mean one with a particular or distinctive feature that marks it out from the standard comprehensive school. It might be its religious character (*e.g.* church schools) or curricular focus (*e.g.* technology schools) or educational philosophy (*e.g.* Steiner schools) or the particular mission it negotiates with an education authority (*e.g.* charter schools). This sector has grown in recent years and is being encouraged and expanded in the United Kingdom by the government of Tony Blair. *Home schooling* has grown dramatically in English-speaking countries in the last decade, but it remains by far the smallest of the three sectors.

It is impossible to predict accurately how the relative size of these sectors might change in the future though I shall be surprised if both specialist schooling and home schooling do not continue to grow. The common secondary school may remain the dominant form of school for the foreseeable future, but in terms of their relative significance on what happens in schools and in society, I think we should reverse the present rank order with home schooling at the top, and specialist schools next, with the comprehensive in third place.

The challenge of home schooling

Home schooling is a direct challenge by parents to the very idea of schooling. It marks the ultimate loss of faith by parents in the public school. Why is this occurring? Here are some of the main factors:

- Parents are worried about bullying in school and the way schools might involve their children in delinquency and drug taking. In a recent British survey, nine out of ten parents were worried about the impact on their children of alcohol and drug abuse and three out of four about bullying.

- Educating children at home strengthens family ties and values – schools cannot be trusted to abide by and transmit these values.

- The sort of parents who are increasingly attracted by the merits of home schooling are themselves home workers who make constant use of the new information and communication technologies (ICT). So why send children to schools where ICT facilities are poorer and most teachers are afraid of ICT?

- School teachers were once essential – when they had access to the knowledge and material denied to most parents. ICT gives open access to unimaginable amounts of information and materials; and we are at the beginning of this revolution. By working and learning together, with the parents acting as general coaches rather than detailed instructors, there is a more natural mode of education between parent and child at home, working and learning alongside one another in the natural rhythms of life rather than in the artificial structures of the normal school day and year.

47

- Nor does the child need to be educated wholly at home. Home schoolers are often sophisticated parents, in entrepreneurial types of work, so they readily band together to form consortia that can hire qualified teachers and even premises to supplement the quality of home schooling by teaching provided outside the home but tailored to their particular needs and wholly under their control.

- Most important of all, perhaps, the child educated at home is likely to develop the skills, attitudes and mind-set of self-reliance, adaptability and networking so important in the flexible, self-employed world of work in the next century – and these are attitudes and skills that, despite the official rhetoric, are very difficult to nurture in the conventional school and classroom.

Specialist schools

If home schooling does indeed grow in the way and for the reasons I suggest, then parents will be making that choice against the standard comprehensive or common public school. The existence of the specialist school may well be crucial here and make the choice of home schooling both more difficult and less likely. The specialist school is a powerful protection against the spread of declining faith in public education as well as a nation's best hope for raising levels of achievement. My reason for so suggesting is that specialist schools often have beneficial features:

- In specialist schools, there is a strong partnership between home and school. It has been known for many years that where the parents are interested in and actively support their child's schooling, the child achieves more at school. Specialist schools capitalise on parental as well as student commitment. Communities of shared interest are strong communities and potentially of great importance as the old geographical communities that feed the common school weaken and decay.

- Moreover the specialist school successfully transmits, formally and informally, the values of its community, one which commands the trust of parents.

- Specialist schools find it easier to form a partnership with business and industry that relates to the school's specialism with the employers acting as general benefactors of the schools, encouraging their staff to be in the school as teachers and mentors, and offering work experience and vital job access to the school's students.

- Specialist schools invest in the continuing professional development of their teachers. They are more likely than other schools to contribute to school-based initial teacher training, which gives them advantages in recruiting new teachers, and to become centres for in-service education and continuing professional development to all local teachers of the school's specialism, which enhances the standing and quality of the school's own teachers. Teachers are themselves treated by the school as lifelong learners who are most likely to model this orientation and transmit it to their students.

– Specialist schools are more likely to use focused ICT, especially where there is a curriculum specialty, and to harness the huge potential of ICT at home. The school develops imaginative and inspiring partnerships of teachers and students with a world-wide range of people and institutions through ICT. Networks of schools expand beyond the traditional limitations of time and space into enriching "virtual consortia". The dissemination of innovations between countries begins to take place between schools and teachers in rapid uncontrolled ways, without the aid and consent of local or national education authorities – and perhaps even in spite of them.

The cumulative effect of these factors is to make the specialist school much more effective, in terms of measured cognitive outcomes but also of social outcomes, than the standard common school. In addition, there are some factors built into many specialist schools that encourage innovation in patterns of working in the school and in styles of teaching and learning, making it more flexible and able to adjust to the changing demands that will shape educational institutions in the next century.

Among the most significant are new patterns of staffing schools, including the use of teaching assistants to support fewer but far better qualified and more effective high-grade teachers. The school can also draw upon part-time and seconded staff from the world of work relevant to the school's specialism. Specialist schools are most likely to abandon the factory model of schooling by restructuring the school year, the school term and the school day – especially in ways that encourage independent learning by students and team working on projects. I predict that it is these specialist schools which will most quickly achieve a key (and measurable) structural change, namely a reduction in the number and use of conventional classrooms in favour of other arrangements for individual study and group work based on individual learning plans, not lesson plans for whole classes. In the light of declining use of classrooms, the specialist school can be less rigidly age-graded than the common school, and students mix and work together according to their learning needs, preferences, plans and level of achievement rather than age.

Specialist schools, and technology schools in particular, will soon have pupils using ICT at home for some of the week. It is they who lead the way in "schooling *from* home" (as opposed to home schooling). At the same time, this means that the specialist school is potentially the most responsive one to home schoolers, in that its flexibility enables it to offer the part-time and "customised" schooling that home schoolers want for their children. The school in

Alberta, Canada, described for this seminar, for instance, has used ICT to very good effect to overcome geographical limitations. A school can potentially expand in relation to new demand, either from home schoolers or distant families, well beyond its physical capacity. The conventional comprehensive school will regard home schoolers merely as a threat. Specialist schools are able to pioneer the mix of home schooling and customised, part-time formal schooling out of which a very different school can emerge. They will be among the first to develop into the "neighbourhood learning centres" that many see as a critical feature of lifelong education in the community.

The specialist schools will, in all likelihood, most fully adopt apprenticeship modes of teaching and learning to ensure that students get beyond the instruction-dependent character of conventional schooling which leads many adolescents to become instruction-resistant. As specialist schools, in partnership with some home schoolers, inculcate in their students the mind-set of entrepreneurialism and networking, and attitudes of self-reliance and self-organisation, they prepare the students *both* for the changing world of employment *and* for lifelong learning. The two are inextricably linked.

Most important of all, the specialist school is the seedbed of the school as a learning organisation and a *knowledge-creating* organisation. Schools are resilient institutions; they are highly resistant to change, as so many reformers – whether they be Ministers of Education or school principals – have found to their cost. In the next century schools will have to be highly responsive to changing circumstances and needs. They will, I believe, be able to this only if, through their partnerships and their responsiveness to those partners, they are able to create the knowledge to allow them to evolve into the new forms and patterns required. Specialist schools are particularly well placed to achieve the degree of responsive flexibility by which they can evolve rapidly in ways that may well make the school of 2020 barely recognizable in terms of what most schools are like today.

Whither the inner-city common school?

Not all schools will have these capacities. Indeed, I fear that the standard comprehensive school, especially ones serving areas of relative disadvantage in the inner-city, will usually trail behind the specialist school in its capacity to respond creatively to the pressures for change and, at its worst, will be unequal to the challenge. Many countries have for many years sought to engineer enhanced effectiveness in the inner-city schools, which have proved to be highly resistant to long-term or sustained improvement, despite both the undoubted dedication of many principals and teachers and the commitment of governments, which has included the creation of education action zones with additional resources. Why are they likely to be less responsive than the specialist schools to the impending pressures on schools? Here are some possible explanations:

– they cannot respond adequately to young people's need for jobs and specific preparation for such jobs;

– they tend to be low in attractiveness to the best qualified and more competent teachers and headteachers;

– students lack essential high quality ICT in their homes;

– ICT in school is used for entertainment and containment rather than education;

– this "custodialism" handicaps students because it cannot give them the attitudes and skills (initiatives, self-reliance, the capacity to learn on-the-job) needed in the new climate of work and employment;

– the school fails to inculcate the mix of imagination and entrepreneurial skills that generates the work ethic to replace the employment ethic and provide the key element of community regeneration in disadvantaged areas;

– in consequence, the school is weak in its preparation of students for lifelong learning;

– because of weak community structure and dysfunctional households, and the associated problems of poverty, crime and drugs, teachers' efforts to provide civic and moral education through the curriculum (not the direct experience of community available in specialist schools) tend to fail;

– only parents who cannot (or choose not to) opt into other sectors (specialised schools, home schooling, private schools) send their children to these schools;

– which thus become "under-class" schools, reproducing their parents, namely the unemployed or casual unskilled labour.

The persisting problem of the inner-city common school and its impact on social exclusion will help to stimulate governments to review policies for educational change and improvement. My assumption is that over the next two or three decades schools will need to innovate in the light of the deep and linked changes taking place in the three major social institutions – in the world of work; in the structure of families/households; and in the field of information and communication technologies. Today schools and classrooms in different countries look astonishingly alike. All will need to respond to these deep changes, though the rate of change in one or more of these will vary from country to country. All countries will, therefore, need to invest in educational innovation to overcome the incapacity of schools to respond rapidly and effectively.

51

Investing in educational innovation

Countries are not equal, however, in their capacity to invest in educational innovation at school level. For, such investment is not simply a matter of political will or the availability of resources, relevant though both these are. Some countries have structural features that will promote or inhibit the right kind of educational investment. It is important to ask, at national government level, at regional/local government/education authority level and at school level:

– what are the *predispositions* to innovation?

– what are the *pressures* towards innovation?

– what are the *potentialities* for innovation?

By *predispositions*, I mean both the structures which lend themselves to innovation and also the dispositional readiness to engage in or to encourage and support new ideas, to tolerate difference, to experiment. A key feature here is the extent of diversity already built into the education system. In some countries, such as the Netherlands, there is a relatively long-standing commitment to diversity of schools and to specialist schools; in many others, either the common or comprehensive school is dominant, or there is a selective system with an associated but severely restricted variety of schools. Diversified systems tend to offer greater parental choice of schools than less diversified ones. Diversity thus entails the acceptance of innovation at school level but central control is weaker. Monolithic systems are more easily controlled, but innovative urges at school level are more frequently stifled.

Education systems also vary along the dimensions of centralisation/decentralisation, in matters such as finance, curriculum and decision-making. This has been a key feature of recent reforms, and in some countries there has been an increase in both centralisation (*e.g.* in curriculum) and decentralisation (*e.g.* in financial delegation). It may be, of course, that some countries are more favourably disposed, at government level, to look outside their own borders for innovative ideas and practices – or just different ones, for what is standard practice in one country is an innovation elsewhere. (Surprisingly little is known, however, about how to transfer or transplant an educational practice from one country or culture to another: we have yet to work out what I might call an educational transfer immunology.)

By *pressures*, I mean forces which are likely to drive the actors at one or more of the three levels to engage in innovative educational activity, even despite personal antipathy to innovation. Some countries have outstanding records for the quality of their vocational education and partnership with employers (*e.g.* Germany), whereas in other countries there has been deep suspicion of vocational education before the end of compulsory education (*e.g.* the United States, the United Kingdom). In the former, employers are likely to pressure schools to be responsive to their changing needs, whereas in the latter, schools can remain resistant to employer demands. Again, in some countries there is a wide gap between rich and poor, between majority and minority ethnic groups, between the old and the young. The degree of social polarisation and the extent of social exclusion may serve as pressures towards educational innovation.

By *potentialities*, I mean those factors which make it easier for a country to engage, at one or more of the three levels, in the kind of innovation that is likely to be needed over the coming years. In some countries there is strong interest in, and provision for, ICT in schools, which in consequence are well placed to capitalise on ICT as an agent of institutional change.

From these different predispositions, pressures and potentialities, hypotheses can be generated about innovation. Some obvious hypotheses would include:

- the greater the degree of school diversity and specialisation, the greater the predisposition to innovate at school and classroom levels;
- the greater the extent of decentralisation, the greater the predisposition to innovate at school and classroom levels;
- the greater the degree of parental choice, the greater the pressure for innovation to meet parental preferences at school and education authority levels;
- the lower the parental satisfaction with school provision, the greater the pressure for innovation;
- the greater the assigned importance of, and provision for, ICT in schools, the greater the potentiality for innovation;
- the greater the social polarisation and social exclusion in a society, the greater the pressure at national level for educational innovation to help to reduce these.

What is far from clear is under what conditions and in which societies such hypotheses might be confirmed. Differences in national cultures and traditions, when combined with the differences in patterns of predispositions, pressures and potentialities, mean that both the extent and form of innovation may differ quite radically from country to country over the next two decades and may be far deeper that we now imagine. The last hundred years have seen relative *convergence* of schooling systems, which is shown in that schools everywhere are very similar. But it is possible that, in the field of education, globalisation will enhance a new *divergence* in schooling systems.

In many countries, the policies for educational innovation at national level are slight and weakly funded. As a proportion of total expenditure on education, there is little investment in educational research and development, at least relative to equivalent investment in, say, industry or medicine – and much of the small budget that exists is devoted to academic research rather than true R&D. Over the last two decades, several countries, perhaps most notably the United States, have engaged in far-reaching, continual educational reform. In almost all countries, Ministries of

Education are clarifying their aims, increasing the goals that schools are now expected to achieve, and then introducing relevant reforms. Some countries have become well practised in reform, which does not mean that they are equally well practised in innovation. Reform is "top-down" and large-scale and does not necessarily entail very much change in how teachers and students experience schooling and what they do in classrooms. So there are limits to reform, especially where, as has become the custom in some countries, reform is initiated without the advantage of any preliminary trials to check their impact on changing for the better what teachers and students do.

Innovation and reform

Governments need to complement their urge to reform – and their inclination, when reform does not work, simply to reform some more – with policies for innovation. For innovation is mostly "bottom-up" and small-scale, it is what the imaginative and responsive school does when it encounters problems and challenges or when it thinks out a different and potentially better way of doing something that has become staled by custom or tradition. There need to be policies and resources that are directed to such innovation. It is from this that the schools will inventively fashion and evaluate the new educational designs that the centre can later, where appropriate, disseminate through the system – possibly as a reform. "Top-down" reform without "bottom-up" innovation will not, I suggest, create the schools we need for tomorrow's world. Under government-led policies and resources for innovation, schools might develop the courage and creativity to innovate and thereby help the government to achieve the right balance and sequence between reform and innovation.

Some of this innovation will not be where governments first look for change – in mainstream schools. In our search for the schools of tomorrow we might learn a lesson from the evolutionary biologists, who tell us not to think of evolution as a matter of linear progression. New species tend to emerge from small, peripheral populations which may overtake the mainstream populations affected by adverse factors. Mainstream schools may face serious challenges in the years ahead; what is happening in the more peripheral areas of the education service may be a better indicator of what is to survive as tomorrow's mainstream school. (At the Hiroshima seminar, Korea's Yungsan Sung-Jee School and Japan's Harumi Junior High School are striking examples of interesting, idiosyncratic schools at the periphery of mainstream schooling.) We have some control over the evolution of educational institutions, though it may mean fostering innovation lavishly, for we cannot now gauge what, in ten or more years' time, is likely to work best in what will be different social and economic circumstances. Since education authorities cannot know in advance what school structures and cultures will be needed in 2020 and beyond that, the prudent course is to let the schools themselves search for this much-needed knowledge and test out, through innovation, what works in new conditions.

The much-abused term "learning organisation" is clearly relevant to the innovative school. It cannot mean merely that the school adopts ideas from outside itself, but rather that it has the capacity to create its own knowledge in its response to the challenges it faces. An important analysis of what this might mean is provided by Nonaka and Takeuchi (1995). The book is about business and seeks to explain why Japanese companies have been so effective in continuous incremental innovation and to that end offers a revolutionary thesis about the knowledge-creating organisation as a key to the innovation needed in crisis circumstances. The thesis remains to be applied to schools.

Knowledge creation is a hazardous, even dangerous, process as well as a difficult one. The speed of social and economic change accelerates; the scale of the educational challenge rises in proportion. Creating the knowledge to generate radical innovation of school level will involve considerable risk-taking if it is to be innovation adequate to meet the challenge. Neither education authorities nor ministers are natural risk-takers – and for understandable reasons. It is school principals and teachers who will be the risk-takers, the calculated risk-takers, out of which the new schools and new educational practices will arise. It can be a painful as well as an exhilarating experience.

This does not mean that during these profound changes there will be no continuities or stabilities in education systems. There may be differences in this regard between primary and secondary education and between East and West. All children need to master basic literacy and numeracy before they are seven or eight years old and this will not decline as a priority in the primary phase of education. In some Eastern countries there has been greater success in this regard and a sounder, evidence-based technology of teaching has emerged for basic literacy and numeracy, whereas in Western teaching of the basics there have been both a weaker evidence base and (at least until very recently) marked differences among teachers in their pedagogy. At secondary level, Western countries can build upon existing conceptions of professional autonomy to encourage innovation in teaching and school design, whereas the Eastern countries may have to take more radical action to stimulate innovation.

Keeping track of innovation and change

From an international perspective, it will be important to track how, over the next two or three decades, countries:

- *Respond to the challenges of lifelong education, changes in the nature of employment, the emergence of new information and communication technologies, changing relationships between home and school, etc.*: will some countries make a more rapid and effective response than others in the way they both conceptualise the educational challenge to schools and introduce changes in policies for educational innovations?

55

– *Vary in their development of policies for school innovation*: will some countries seek to determine and control innovation centrally through direction and legislation whereas other countries stimulate widespread innovation at local and school levels?

– *Move from reform to innovation*: will some countries move from the centralised reform of whole systems – which governments are reluctant to evaluate because failures and mistakes cannot be admitted – to decentralised piece-meal innovations? These can be evaluated without threat and then disseminated when their value and effectiveness is evidenced, as a more prudent approach to managing the changes in schooling needed for the next century. Will there be in some countries a significant shift at ministerial level from controlling and directing to enabling and empowering?

– *Discover the dynamics of successful innovative schools*: will it be possible to move beyond current conceptions of school improvement to a model of schools as knowledge-creating institutions?

– *Learn how to identify promising approaches to school innovation and define criteria by which schools are judged to be effective or exemplary*: will there be a movement away from the focus on a narrow range of measurable, short-term, cognitive outcomes towards less tangible, longer-term, personal and social outcomes? Will criteria of effectiveness vary between the primary and secondary phases of schooling?

– *Develop sophisticated systems for disseminating successful innovation*: will there emerge a middle way between imposing change through legislated reforms and leaving it to schools and teachers to make their individual response to innovations? Will some countries develop more effective systems for the dissemination and implementation of new structures, cultures and practices than has been achieved in the past?

– *Learn how to learn about developing school systems*: are there some countries that will acquire the knowledge and skill of learning how to learn quickly and effectively from other countries? Will that put such countries at the leading edge of effective education?

Unresolved tensions

It is a well-regarded custom for writers and academics in the field of education to adopt what might be termed a "critique-cum-advocacy" approach. That is to say, one offers a critical analysis of some policy or practice, some theory or research, and then advocates an alternative that is held to improve what has been criticised. The object of the analysis is to point to a better way of doing educational work and thus to look constructively to the future.

A different approach is to start from where a society or education system is now, with all the strengths and weaknesses of current policy and practice, and then extrapolate from current trends to possible or likely future developments. This requires one to suspend, temporarily, one's strongly held values and preferences lest what one desires clouds one's perception of what might be. It is a form of analysis that is also potentially upsetting for those readers who are used to (and often prefer) a more conventional advocacy. This tension between what we *want* to happen and what we *fear* might happen is quickly exposed in studies of the future.

Predicting the growth of home schooling will please those who favour it and alarm those who fear it, but my prediction is based on my reading of sociological currents, not my own favour or fear. What I think might happen to the inner-city comprehensive school is not what I want to happen. Many of us hoped that the various schemes of educational priority areas or zones that have been tried over the last thirty years would have solved this problem, but any success has been short-term and limited. The gap between the "best" and "worst" schools has tended to grow in recent years, and as OECD countries have pursued policies to develop excellence in education, the task of striving for greater equity has sometimes become less salient than in the past (see Papadopoulos, 1994). Predicting that the trend will continue, though now also driven and shaped by some different forces, can help to uncover why these schools persist as problems. When, after the analysis of possible futures, we resume our values, we may have gained some insights that allow us to examine these as yet unresolved tensions, as well possible solutions to them, in a fresh or more resolute way. Here is one more aid to policy-makers and practitioners as they plan the future of schooling.

Chapter 4

Innovation in Education: Managing the Future?

by

Françoise Cros
Institut national de recherche pédagogique (INRP), France

Introduction

Issues of innovation and change have occupied centre stage in most countries since approximately the end of the Second World War. Despite such attention, the questions they have raised continue to be delicate and complex. That is what makes this such an intriguing subject, as it embraces virtually all the basic issues in education. Innovation for whom and why? Which aspects of education systems need to change? How should changes be implemented and using what resources? What role should be allocated to the various players, on what time scale? Above all, why is it so difficult to change educational institutions, and in particular the practices of teachers? Asking these questions is automatically to ask about the major dimensions of education, including the curriculum, relationships between actors, and the impact of education. The question of transforming systems of education is complex as it raises the nature of control over the future of our societies. More countries are spending higher proportions of their GDP on education: for what purpose? What do they hope to gain? What will the return on investment be? Is it possible to build a fairer society with a high standard of culture by changing the education system? How should we go about this?

All of these questions are fundamental to any society, and go beyond those relating to classroom practices. In this chapter, these questions are addressed in three broad ways. First, the chapter seeks to identify the general conceptions of the management of change in education over the last fifty years, particularly as revealed through policies in different countries. Second, it seeks to arrive at a more precise understanding of the notion of innovation in education and training, particularly through comparison with other examples of innovation, reform, renewal and overall change. Third, there is the wider use of innovations, and the roles they play in altering the course of change in education. This raises a further question: is it possible to anticipate and shape the future of education, when education itself exerts a degree of influence over the society of the future?

Policies for innovation

The globalisation of the economy is necessitating that countries exchange ideas and discover one another.[3] This accelerating phenomenon is overturning vernacular cultures and placing countries' political choices under the microscope. There has been a convergence of education policies and a mutual influence of the different countries confronted by these choices. This can be seen, for instance, in the spread of innovation in east European countries since the fall of the Berlin Wall, as an expression of liberal economics, capitalism and plural democracy.

Innovation is the child of competitive economics; it was born in its current form towards the end of World War II, and is synonymous with a society developing an entrepreneurial spirit embracing risk-taking, creativity and imagination. In contrast, in the Middle Ages innovation was viewed as a calamity, engendering evil and challenging the stability of institutions, particularly that of churches, through the substitution of secular for religious forces. Humankind was thereby developing the ability to create, previously the preserve of God, and hence the nature of society was being overturned. Human beings were becoming autonomous and presenting their opinions, indeed their originality, as a resource that left behind the established social order. Individuals came instead to stand at the centre as the subject of their own futures and of the society they were building. Underpinning the individual was the idea of scientific and technological progress as that took root, and, in parallel, that of social progress. If consumption is developed, and therefore enterprises, so ran the theory, it will be good for humankind. However, recent history has called this comforting model into question.

Three conceptions of policies for innovation in education

Innovation began to make a profound impression on education and training during the 1950s. Before that, to be sure, there had been the great pedagogues such as Rousseau, Pestalozzi, Dewey, Freinet and Montessori, who were innovators and invented new systems of education. But, they were largely marginalised and marginal to the rest of the education system. In France, it was not until the 1960s that the word "innovation" began to appear in official education documentation; previously, there had only been timid references to experimentation and école nouvelle. It was about this time that CERI was set up within the OECD, and since then it has been possible in Western countries to identify three periods during which innovation has been embraced by politicians and the population at large, identified through analysis of official documentation available in France (Cros, 1996).

The background to the first period – approximately the 1960s and 1970s – was that education had served as the guardian of tradition, responding only to gradual change and to the impact of external events. Then, unforeseen developments caused governments to introduce reforms in part to re-establish national hegemony, as for example in the United States when the Russian Sputnik was successfully launched. The period was simultaneously marked by the implementation of a large number of innovations at the grass-roots level. These were often at odds with the wishes of governments, which tended to launch broad-based reforms that were impossible to implement and which regarded the appropriate role of teachers to be to apply meticulously the reforms drawn up by the authorities. It was also the beginning of the "glorious years" of economic development. Innovation ran counter to the axioms articulated by these official choices, founded as they were on reform. Innovation gave the appearance of breaking the mould, suggesting a promise of an alternative society. Governments tended to ignore it and instead introduced the reforms they thought necessary, amidst fanfares of publicity and a plethora of official documentation.

The second period covers the 1980s. The yearning for democracy had become stronger and with particular emphasis on the role of citizens. Yet, it was also a period of uncertainty marked, in the United States, by the humiliations of the Iran hostage crisis, a second, more severe oil slump, and economic recession triggered by international competition. The sense of crisis found expression in an American government report on education entitled "A Nation at Risk". Human resources were now highly valued – all persons were urged to place their intelligence and inventiveness at the service of the nation to assist in the expansion of the education system and develop the future talents as the country's raw material. Innovation was now seen much more positively. It was to be promoted and encouraged, both through direct measures and through incentives. Policies were introduced promoting a series of training initiatives; examples in France included the Missions académiques de la formation des personnels de l'éducation nationale (academic missions for the training of national education staff), and innovatory activities that were piloted and financed by the state. In this case, an innovation "network" occupied a major place in, and helped to regulate, education policy. It was a time when countries with centralised economies were embracing, to a greater or lesser extent, a larger measure of decentralisation.

The third period extends from the early 1990s to the present day. Innovation is no longer simply encouraged, it has become an imperative of professional endeavour. Change in education is being carried out by actors within the system, and mainly by teachers. New ideas and different ways of dealing with problems are coming from teachers themselves, and it is they who are creating most of the innovatory situations for learning and development. It is now for the government to harness these varied achievements and to encourage their widespread use. This is more a question of developing an innovative spirit among the employees working in education than in issuing instructions. "Learning how to learn" is taking place on a broad scale, and methodological acquisition has become more important than content. Participating in innovation comes to be seen as a form of vocational accomplishment warmly encouraged by the authorities as part of the professional repertoire of all teachers.

Alongside these three periods are three conceptions of change found in the political arena. The first is based on the idea that change in the education system relies on official injunctions to announce what has to be done. State employees are supposed to carry out these orders. This conception entails numerous, detailed reforms implemented by and through immutable timetables decided by governments. The education system is expected to keep pace with the changes called for in national policies, and path-breaking ideas are expressed through innovations that would otherwise be rejected or ignored by the school institutions.

The second conception acknowledges that social systems do not change just like that. As Michel Crozier observed in the 1970s, "society cannot be changed by decree". There is a need for a minimum level of commitment on the part of personnel to use the ideas that they themselves have articulated, to understand and channel them in certain directions. In other words, policies use innovations to help give them direction – to promote some developments and discourage others – with official bodies relying on innovations to help steer the education system in their preferred directions.

In the third conception, where political leadership is seen as incapable of arriving at consensus on clear, common projects, it is left to grass-roots initiatives and local innovations to express themselves, and even for them to stamp out innovations that obviously run counter to generally agreed values. Innovations are therefore seen as an everyday practice in all schools, bringing with that practice the obligation to innovate in the face of a changing, demanding society yet where no one knows exactly what future directions that society will take.

The first conception of change seeks to guide change prescriptively through reforms; the second allows the actors more room as long as they embrace what the institution sees as desirable; and the third is based on the free rein of innovators' imaginations and internal arrangements that encourage the play of all forces, even contradictory ones, in the absence of clear political directions. It can be seen that these three stages parallel the progress of an individual innovation. First, it is held aloft as an ideal of the future, then it negotiates its conditions for existence within educational institutions, and finally it is normalised through institutionalisation and becomes part of the fabric of what is taught on a daily basis.

These dynamics can be witnessed in many countries, particularly in Europe. The third conception suits innovation best because it is closest to our present-day representations of innovation and to the social fabric of local demands. It may well be the fuse to undermine any national orientation for education, though to suppose that the third phase marks the end of dialogue between political leadership and local situations would not be warranted. Most innovations currently being developed in Western countries originate among actors who have "interpreted" national political directions, through negotiations and interplay between official policies and grass-roots issues. Innovation therefore emerges as the outcome of a "knitting together" of the opportunities identified by innovators themselves.

National policies for innovation

The first task of the European Observatory of Innovations in Education and Training (referred to in Note 3) was to identify governments' different conceptions of the management of innovation. Clearly, it is difficult to make comparisons, given the disparities between countries concerning culture, language and history. Certain trends nevertheless emerge.[4] These may be analysed on three levels: structural, thematic, and in terms of the actors.

At the *structural* level, it is well-known that some countries like Germany (with its *Länder*) and England are very decentralised, while others, like France and Greece, are relatively centralised. Over the last ten years, however, there has been a movement towards decentralisation in strongly centralised countries, and a contrary movement towards centralisation in the decentralised countries like Denmark and England, with its relatively recent detailed National Curriculum. This re-balancing or "re-centring" serves to undermine the situation whereby an innovation develops its own local voice while at the same time relying on an official representative to provide resources or offer general orientations. These "re-centring" shifts instead underline the major role to be played by intermediary roles and spaces, that lie between national officials, on one side, and the teachers, on the other. Such intermediaries may be inspectors, advisers, trainers or school principals.

Such arrangements are consistent with the notion of innovations emerging in concrete ways through particular actors backed by a concern for support, assistance and facilitation, without that necessarily entailing control. In France, however, the confusion of roles, whereby inspectors both make evaluations and give advice, can inhibit the spread of innovations. For the intermediary to be effective in the innovation process they should not be in a hierarchical relation with the school or teacher. There is growing recognition of the actors' imaginations as the instigators of innovations and the sources of change, while not leaving them entirely on their own. They can draw on intermediary bodies likely to help them and network these innovations in such a way as to give them coherence and resonance, acting as "levers". It is as if grass-roots innovations were able to help determine and define policy directions for changing the education system.

In this context, we can question the rather simplistic "top-down" *vs* "bottom-up" contrast often used to grasp the link between the national and local, as innovation really lies somewhere "in between", depending on the stage it has reached. Originally, an innovation derives from the grass roots, and therefore, providing it continues

63

at all, has no link with official bodies, and is instead in close proximity with the local situation. As it gradually moves away from the grass roots pursuing its own momentum and analysis, it comes to occupy a more substantial place in negotiations and exchanges with intermediaries, thereby assuming a role in networks oriented towards the national level. At each stage, there is interaction back and forth which, if the intermediary plays its role well, becomes part of a more distanced (and less grass-roots) process operating at the regional, or even national, level. This is one of the conceptions of institutionalisation examined below.

On the *thematic* level: research carried out by the Observatory focused on themes prioritised by the European Union for the transformation of the education system, namely, equal opportunities, the learning of languages and cultural mediation, and staff training. All of these themes are to be found in countries' policies, though often interpreted differently. An issue such as equal opportunities may also be understood in relatively similar ways in different countries, but its theoretical bases and underpinnings are not clear. The themes of innovations may, however, be identified through examination of practice: the integration of problem or disabled pupils into ordinary schools (particularly in Italy, and in Great Britain, Ireland, Spain and France, according to the Observatory); the implementation in some countries of measures specifically dealing with ethnic minorities (Greece and Portugal); and measures in yet other countries designed to combat early drop out from school. Two issues appear to be particular priorities – equal opportunities and teacher training – while other themes raised through the Observatory have included the autonomy of educational establishments and changing the curriculum. Information and communications technology is important in all countries, and deserves serious study in itself.

The actors: policies take increasing account of the local dimension, and of the influence exerted not only by local authorities but also by parents as education consumers. The directions taken therefore often derive from local negotiations which have already taken innovations on board. Many actors are thus becoming aware of innovations that no longer remain exclusive to teachers. The role of partnership has gained ground with the greater opening of the education system. This is found, for instance, in Japanese local authorities and prefectures with parental involvement in the drive to promote more imaginative and creative education.

All together, innovation is shifting from a location in central political institutions to a range of actors with the re-working of the social fabric. Innovation becomes local property, yet teachers face a dynamic which requires them not simply to turn in on internal school-based preoccupations, but to embrace new possibilities relating to culture and citizenship, and the creation of diverse networks.

The meaning of innovation in education and training

The notion of innovation has many meanings – it is part of a common, "floating" language. It is the subject of intense negotiations between the various parties of a given institution. At the same time, it offers the promise of hope and a still better future; it has almost mystical qualities. We commonly regard it as beneficial, but the example of the innovation represented by the invention of the guillotine in France, permitting greater efficiency in putting people to death, shows that it need not imply improvement. Even so, the dominant association is positive. Not to innovate is regarded as synonymous with conservatism, stultification, backwardness and loss of dynamism.

To address the meaning of innovation in relation to education, it is useful to review both surveys of how it is understood, and more theoretical considerations. The work by the European Observatory of Innovations has shown how variable are the connotations of the word "innovation", not only from one country to the next, but also between people in the same country. It is a term that we can imagine invokes broad agreement, but in fact it gives rise to different, and even opposing, intellectual and emotional reactions. Despite this variation, there is a common substratum core meaning we identified in the course of this research. This we have termed a "paradigm" – a series of ideas and opinions structured within a relatively common culture (*i.e.* democratic economic capitalism) and shared by a group of individuals (in this case, the government representatives interviewed), which enables us both to understand and have an influence on the world around us.

The innovation paradigm is widely supported in the countries of the European Union, although a degree of disenchantment may be detected in some places, possibly, for example, Germany.[5] Four main ideas make up this common paradigm: *i*) the idea of the new and novel; *ii*) the idea of addressing unmet social needs and values; *iii*) the issue of power; and *iv*) the idea of change.

- *The idea of the new.* The new is seen as a form of creativity: "innovation is a new, creative solution in education policy", "a creative way of renewing education", "the creation of a new culture in education" and "a new idea for overcoming certain problems in education" (Finland). Also, "it is a creative process that makes a clean break with established paradigms" (Ireland), and involves "the government and education leaders in creating ways of increasing pupils' equal opportunities" (the Netherlands). Alongside this idea of creation lies that of newness on its own; it is seen to entail a new situation in which "one departs from routines in order to take risks and discover life" (Ireland). Newness plays a key role in defining innovation, even though some people entertain doubts about how often innovations are truly original or even whether this is necessary.

- *The idea of addressing unmet social needs and values.* Innovation appears to guarantee the concrete implementation of commended values: "Reform is based on principles (*e.g.* democratisation and equal opportunities), and innovation is a measure for carrying it out and guaranteeing quality" (Observatory, Spain). Behind innovation lies the possibility of giving concrete expression in schools to democratic aspirations such as equal opportunities: "Innovation is all about government and education leaders creating ways of achieving equal opportunities for young people" (Austria). A more recent value, quality, has emerged in countries like the Netherlands, Belgium, England and Spain. Another reason for the existence of innovation is that it improves what is already in existence and optimises aims assigned to the education system (France and Ireland). Most countries see innovation as an energising value. Only in a minority were doubts expressed, whether about the positive associations of innovation in general or about actual beneficial effects. In Austria, for example, "stability and harmony are highly valued; by contrast, reform and change, which are marked by potential conflicts, have a latent, negative connotation".

– *The idea of power.* Because innovation is supported by values and educational objectives does not mean that the latter are all consistent. Conflicts of values are linked to conflicts of power. In fact, borrowing from the writings of Alain Touraine, we might say that there is a struggle for historicity through education, that is to say for the cultural control of the nation. Governments put their credibility on the line when it comes to education, and have no wish to be destabilised by minority currents based on powerful mould-breaking values.

Innovation is not the property of either the grass roots or the government. It may be defined as an intelligent mixture of negotiations, contracts and decisions which take place more or less smoothly, according to the size and nature of the country in question. There is widespread agreement that innovation introduces uncertainty into centre/periphery relationships.

– *The idea of change.* In views gathered from most European countries, innovation is all about changing behaviour, attitudes, approaches and ways of thinking. It is also a process of steady evolution in line with continuity, linked to "a development and enhancement of the system" (Observatory, Germany). Innovation appears in situations of transition or questioning, when the authorities and individuals no longer know if education still guarantees certain values or what their role is in education (as with churches in some countries). This is a case of intermittent change in which an example of innovation may "lead to a variety of stages and dimensions" (Ireland). Austria is undergoing "top-down" changes; education reform "does not involve the education system making a permanent adjustment to the new needs of a democratic society; rather it consists of occasional major pieces of legislation followed by long periods of consolidation during which schools are supposed to be left in peace". Similarly, in England, people are described as losing interest in innovation because it is an unending process that causes fatigue and exhaustion.

66

In other words, in all European countries there is agreement that innovation is change, but recognition too that this change cannot be continual because of the danger of "burn out" and the possibility that a process that is no longer innovatory can turn into a routine. A form of innovation is born, it lives and dies, it spreads far afield or it becomes marginalised, it takes hold or it disappears. When we speak of ongoing innovation, we mean the birth of numerous improving innovations together with their extension or institutionalisation. Some countries in Europe do not use the word "innovation" at all, or else they challenge it. Some correspondents went so far as to suggest that innovation may be a way of introducing a typically European form of management. Examples here include German-speaking countries and Denmark, which speak of "innovation as a new concept in the context of Denmark" that Europe has imported, and Austria where the word is felt to be a "technical term" used in research policy, or an "anglicism channelling the German language through an international corpus of knowledge introduced by bodies such as the OECD".

The theoretical basis

When, as social science researchers, we analyse innovation in education and research, we have to define the issue and its field of application (see Cros, 1998). In this section, the main elements of the term are analysed as it has passed from idea to concept, defined operationally. Innovation can have four powerful, non-contingent internal attributes: the idea of new; the phenomenon of change; the final action; and the process:

- *The idea of new.* As this has already been mentioned, the treatment here can be brief. Newness in innovation is in relation to the immediate context and to the context that articulates it. For example, "new" may be something old that has been restored. Similarly, bringing the Internet into the classroom is no guarantee of the presence of innovation. It is possible to use very modern tools within an extremely traditional teaching method. Newness on its own does not ensure innovation.

- *The phenomenon of change.* This, too, has already been referred to. Innovation is change, but not all change is innovation. For there to be innovation, there needs to be a voluntary, deliberate and intentional element.

- *The final action.* This has been considered in reference to values. An innovation brings values through an action that has objectives. These values may differ from those defended by present-day institutions, and this explains why innovation may lead to conflicts of values or of power. An innovation may only be partly identified with a particular project. Like the project, it has objectives, but it is not governed by a programme or a timetable; it is subject to the unpredictable hazards of the action, to uncertainties, to discoveries and to retreats. An innovation is also made up of surprises that have to be dealt with on a day-to-day basis, and quite often it achieves objectives that were not assigned to it at the outset.

– *The process*. This expands the above observations made about the uncertain final action, the product of a spiral series of events that were unexpected and sequential, that build upon the effects of different perceptions and experiences of time of the main actors. In other words, innovation can only flow from the actors themselves so that the authorities can only leave the actors margins of freedom so that they can react by inventing actions that are more appropriate and closer to the actual situation. A reform may therefore be a way of enabling actors to innovate, and this permits them to take a number of initiatives, protected from conservative pressures by official documentation within a defined framework.

Often, the only innovations that experts are familiar with are no more than cases written up to a broadly common format. A grid has been established by the Observatory to make this more systematic. It has four dimensions:

– The rationale for the choice of the innovation (*e.g.* what is innovatory about it, and how it has been implemented).

– A description of the innovation in terms of such factors as objectives, the people affected, the size of the innovation and its duration.

– The account of the introduction of the innovation, its strategies and its operation.

– An analysis of the innovation as regards process (*e.g.* initiative, different stages, decisive moments, development of networks, obstacles and sources of support) and evaluation. This should include examination of those conducting the survey and their methods of inquiry.

Analysis according to this grid provides a good general idea of what the innovation is about but it will still be a pale reflection of the much richer and more complex reality. To get round such limitations, experts can refer in addition to one or two people who are close to the innovation, who present it with enthusiasm and portray its positive aspects. It should be recognised that such advocates are there to promote the innovation as a product, and not to give it calm consideration, and this raises complex issues of values and of power that, in the context of conferences for instance, are difficult to avoid. Innovation is a most difficult idea to work with if one wants to steer clear of the partisan.

However, in the light of case studies, such as those prepared for the Observatory and for the Hiroshima seminar, analyses of innovations are becoming more numerous and connected. Not so long ago, case studies were focused largely on innovations that were clearly targeted and isolated within a school; now the whole school and beyond are involved. This in turn raises important questions: do growing numbers and inter-connections mean that innovation can have a more wide-ranging impact? Can we identify the birth of what we might call a "culture of innovation"?

The effects of innovation on education and training

In this section, we shall examine conceptions of the expansion of innovation *en route* to asking if there are political "systems" and practices that are better suited to the spread and propagation of innovation than others. To address this suggests a preliminary question: what do those who wish to disseminate innovations want to achieve? In discussions with innovatory practitioners, very few of them talk about disseminating their innovations because they are too busy setting them up. A survey conducted by the French Ministry of Education contained a question on the transferability of innovation. The replies contained little profound reflection, referring simply to the factors needed for an innovation to survive, such as financial resources and confidence on the part of senior administrators in educational institutions who implement education policies. Such administrators are concerned with the dissemination of innovations but not all innovations – only those they consider worth promoting. What does disseminating an innovation in a school mean? Does an innovation disseminate itself? Research has described the idea of transferring an innovation as a failure; a study of French colleges has identified the limited impact of research outcomes on changes in educational establishments (Demailly, 1991). An innovation is not transposed without the process starting up again, that is to say without a vital transformation in which everyone, for his/her own benefit, has to re-invent a new way of working together in a socially constructed space.

Different conceptions of the generalisation of innovation

Over the last 20 years, social science researchers have based their work on generalisation of three models developed by American researchers in the 1960s, that have now become classic:

- *Research-development-dissemination-adoption*. This model is based on the economic, industrial conception of innovation as a technical innovation, assuming linear rationality, planning and the division of labour. During the 1970s, attempts were made to develop education research and apply results at the grass roots according to this model.

- *Social interaction based on communication between individuals*. This is discussed in more detail later as this conception has since been extended and developed.

- *Solving problems with the user as starting-point*. This is an ecological approach to innovation based on an analysis of professional practices, broadened by new ways of thinking.

69 |

Contemporary models, more sensitive to the complexity of innovation, have developed alongside these three classic models. They may be grouped into four types:

– the epidemiological model;

– the social interactionism model;

– the institutionalisation model;

– the action-research model.

The epidemiological model

An initial approach to innovation in the 1980s was based on epidemiology, but this did not take firm root (Mendras, 1983, pp. 75-76). It has been taken up again more recently by American anthropologists (Sperber, 1996). The epidemiological paradigm is based on the idea that innovation will spread, in a given population, in the same way as a cholera epidemic. The general dissemination paradigm is represented by an S-shaped logistic curve, which is cumulative as growing numbers of people are "touched". The first people to be "touched" are the pioneers, followed by a gradually increasing number of people until the entire population has been affected. Such a statement begs many questions: what makes one innovation spread better than another? What is the profile of "pioneers"?

Research has sought to identify the characteristics of innovators/pioneers to conclude:

– innovators have a higher standard of education than the population as a whole;

– they come from a higher social class, or else they are moving up the social scale;

– they listen to, watch and read news media;

– they take part in social demonstrations (*e.g.* through associations, trade unions, political parties or voluntary action);

– they have greater than average empathy skills and high ambitions;

– they are sympathetic to change in general, and support education and knowledge.

Age is not relevant as, contrary to a widely held view, it is possible to innovate at any age. The innovator who enjoys an elevated status can become an opinion-former and play a role in legitimating opinion. These characteristics are coveted by others, and endow innovators with a charisma that contributes to the adoption of an innovation.

However, the characteristics of the innovator are not the only factors involved in the contagion. It also depends on the characteristics of the innovation itself, including:

- the extent to which the relative benefit of the innovation is visible and therefore convincing (good publicity in support of the innovation is likely to play a decisive role);

- the perception of the innovation's complexity – if the innovation seems to be too complex or complicated, it is likely to be rejected;

- the compatibility of the innovation with the context of the class or school and with the teacher's own competence;

- the extent to which the innovation easily lends itself to experimentation, and can be cut back;

- anyone who has had a painful experience with an innovation will not come back to it quickly, making it particularly important to avoid failure.

This epidemiological conception has been recently taken up again as part of a naturalist theory of culture in which it is the ideas that are contagious, not the practices. The distribution takes place at a symbolic level. People incorporate two universes of thought (or representations): an individual universe linked to the unique experience that each person experiences (mental representations), and an inter-individual universe (public representations) facilitating exchanges. These two universes are dependent and, over the years, can move depending on meetings, expectations and beliefs. The latter are well established in education as they are expressed through principles proclaimed on behalf of education such as "all people are equal" (which is to abandon reason for an option of infinite interpretations, and hence beliefs). Research is under way into these mutual changes of representations and into the prospect of the existence of the "modularity" of thought.

The social interactionism model – the interplay of influences

The epidemiological model allows little room for the wishes or decisions of individuals, as they are assumed to be "infected" in spite of themselves. It focuses mainly on collective movement rather than individuals. Individual decisions and their aggregated effects at a social level lie at the core of the interactionist model. It focuses on mechanisms for persuasion that are slow and complicated to a greater or lesser degree, linked to two key parameters:

- *Given and received information.* This information is recomposed in each person's mind so that it is tolerable and does not excessively endanger his/her own representations as with the fable of the fox and the grapes (the fox is too small and, instead of acknowledging that smallness which is belittling, the fox asserts instead that the grapes are too green).

– *Communications networks, particularly personal networks*. This brings the focus to the very heart of the process of social influence. Someone's interest is awakened, he/she is shown that there is no danger (hence the key role of pioneers), the newness is legitimated by innovators, and others (colleagues, neighbours, friends) confirm and legitimate the innovation.

Social participation provides the individual with the collective support that offers reassurance and security, and fosters the development of the innovation. However, the influence is not free of conflicts or crises and these also bring about change. Other elements involved in the propagation of innovation include the phenomena of conformity, submission to power, the social cost represented by the stigma of being in a minority, and social pressure.

The institutionalisation model

Innovation has a period of duration and, in the best of cases, it leaves a trace of itself behind. When it is adopted by an institution, it becomes appropriated so that the innovation loses its mould-breaking energy and enthusiasm, turns into an element absorbed by the institution, and becomes part of a routine. Education institutions similarly do not remain still but instead evolve. Ministries, for example, are never static, and they embrace a number of foreign elements if they are unlikely to pose a fundamental challenge to them which in turn supply them with the whiff of oxygen needed to ensure their own survival. In other words, they live off an innovation by absorbing it. The innovation is firmly institutionalised when it appears in legislation to which teachers must refer.

Institutionalisation derives from the coming together of the institutional heritage and social acquisitions of the past, on one side, and innovation, on the other, which breathes new life into the institution or person by challenging the established *raison d'être*. Institutionalisation facilitates the necessary agreement without which there would be no society. An innovation that seeks a broad base and wishes to establish itself over a long period in society must undergo this process of institutionalisation which forces it into some restructuring and to an adaptation to the general institutional context. This is a particular dissemination process that has been studied through organisational innovations in enterprises (Alter, 1996). In schooling, it can take place in two stages. First, administrators encourage teachers to support innovation (*e.g.* in pilot experiments, and by giving initiatives their backing); second, directors pursue a policy of institutionalising innovations: they rationalise them, make them compulsory by "normalising" them, and standardise them through the reactions of groups that enjoy legal backing (*e.g.* ministers, heads of academic institutions, inspectors).

It follows that institutionalisation acts as a sorting-out process: at a given moment particular innovations enjoy a position of power, but other issues and innovations may later drive them out. Institutionalisation may also be accelerated. It is always operated by bodies that support the institution's values and are legitimated by it. However, is it possible to imagine an institution so suicidal as to allow revolutionary innovations to develop which then radically question the values on which the institution is founded, even to the point of overturning it?

The action-research model

This dissemination model is based on co-operation between several partners who have philosophies and objectives that are often quite diverse. On the one hand, there is the researcher who may sometimes be seen as a trainer, organiser, consultant or militant; on the other is the practitioner, who may be seen as a social player, partner or client. Action-research is not just a simple juxtaposition of these two sides, but a mutual clarification that helps practice to develop and objectives to be consolidated.

According to Lewin and his followers, the research process is at the service of social change. It is, on this view, a question of applying scientific methodology to the clarification and solution of concrete problems; it is also a process of personal and social change. In both meanings, it constitutes a learning process in which the accent is placed on the quality of the collaboration in planning the action and in evaluating the results (Lewin, 1948, p. 57). As a system for disseminating innovation, action-research assumes, first, that researchers are activists, striving for a particular outcome of social action; second, that innovation is not something that exists outside the practitioner, and is not strictly the adoption or an adaptation of practices developed elsewhere. It is an appropriation by actors, supported by practices that are novel in that context.

A model for disseminating innovation supported by sociology has emerged more recently. This is the "translation" model. Here, innovation is regarded as a complex social construct that brings all the actors into play – institutional actors, new products, innovators, clients, and consumers – around either a common good or a temporary collective interest. Translation can be understood as a mechanism whereby a social world gradually establishes itself and finds stability. It consists of placing a language at the service of an innovation so as to reduce the various networked actors to a single discourse in a given place dealing with a given subject.

The desire to know the future

One reason why innovation is so beguiling is that it carries within it the potential of what is to come. Beyond this, it expresses a will to change. It seems to promise a world that will no longer be chaotic, and instead resemble a beautiful, smooth curve that has been established reasonably in the light of calculated risks. People have always wanted to know about the future – and they have always got it wrong for the unexpected always happens. The future is an abstraction in which we invest our unsatisfied desires and aspirations of paradise. Whatever the futurologists may say, it remains prophecy reliant on conjecture.

73

What is it that urges people to try to build futures that inevitably escape them? Some people try to capture half-glimpsed trends in the present as the starting-point for the plurality of possible values in the future to ask what will education then be like. Sometimes, people desire to break with the present, and imaginative proposals have been made that would see education disappear altogether. Two polar opposites find some support in existing trends (as well as the positions between the poles): education disappearing into a diluted society in a manner akin to that forecast by Ivan Illich, or education building up a separate identity in the form of a sanctuary to social isolation and fragmentation. There are examples of innovations that are consistent with both trends. But who can say with any confidence what will happen in the next century? We can do little more than offer rash hypotheses that are comparisons with the present.

Innovation has a fascination because of the emphasis placed on a whole future that has yet to be built, and which can erase the imperfections of the present. It is preferable, for analytical purposes, to look at the present and the uncertain. In his "Passions of the soul", Descartes wrote about the desire not to see death as an end, but as an opening to the future. The yearning for innovation, and for making use of it, surely conceals a profound desire for immortality on the part of humankind. This search for the education of the future is a concern for ruling interests, as they are keen both to anticipate impending problems, and to address what could be done without necessarily scrutinising current performance too closely. The trees can then conceal the forest!

Innovation can refer both to the best and the worst developments. Restoring corporal punishment into schools in Western countries, for instance, would be an innovation in the sense that it would be new by comparison with the current context and would be "new old". A practice of that sort may be effective insofar as it might show, by means of a short-term evaluation, an impact on student achievement. However, it does not conform to the modern ethic and the idea we have formed of human development. In effect, there is a sorting through of innovations and the selection only of those that conform to the aims of democratic countries, and which develop different, original actions that accord with present-day social complexity and mobility. There are two aspects: conformity with democratic values, and the establishment of original elements inspired by a possible future (concerning for instance "virtual work" or lifelong learning). Should, however, education only serve as "socialisation" for a society considered to be better or should it aim to provide access to universals? How far should education resist the growing preoccupation with the social issues of the day?

Educational and political systems that support innovation

Certain conditions that support the development of innovation emerge from the discussion in this chapter. A major condition is adequate freedom to actors and schools to act in a climate of confidence, and one in which there can be exchange between people acting as intermediaries in innovation support, assistance and the enrichment of knowledge. In other words, an education system should be organised in such a way that schools become places for learning, where all the actors, both adults and young people, are on a path of discovery, research, and creation.

Further, there should be the opportunity for education to build networks that go beyond the immediate vicinity or locality. New information technology helps to enlarge these networks in such a way that young persons may construct their own identity: they are each a citizen of the world, and also belong to a corner of it (*i.e.* a country, a region or a place). These are networks of knowledge and human exchange.

Finally, the common aims should be defined by the very people who have to put them into practice in school. What innovation lacks but needs if it is to flourish is a series of aims that have been negotiated and accepted by all the inhabitants of a country. These aims are linked not only to the universality of certain knowledge, but also the cultural and linguistic particularities of each country. Michel Serres has observed that "all learning [which is what innovation is] is travelling and interbreeding" (Serres, 1991, p. 23). The "interbreeding" society, whether this refers to the mixes of ethnicity, languages, cultures, emotions or societies, is increasingly the setting for innovation.

Part III

POLICIES AND PERSPECTIVES FROM JAPAN

The Japanese chapters obviously do not "represent" developments or ideas from that country (moreover Mr. Sugawa's chapter is his own selection of recent developments in Japan and not an official statement). They do reflect Japanese inputs made at the Hiroshima seminar, in addition to the cases of individual schools that are included in the Appendix to this volume.

Tomiji Sugawa, of the Ministry of Education, Science, Sports and Culture, Japan, presents in Chapter 5 a selection of the main themes and aspects of recent Japanese school reform, emphasising the recommendations of the Central Council for Education, and the priorities for change in elementary, lower and upper secondary schooling. The key themes include the development in school students of individuality, creativity, appreciation of human qualities, and their room to think and reflect. Curriculum and accreditation measures for reform at the upper secondary education level are described.

Akira Ninomiya, Hiroshima University, Japan, outlines many of the outstanding challenges and problems that schools must confront going into the 21st century. Emerging innovative structures and approaches to learning are often direct responses to these challenges. Schools as a whole, however, must come to be inspired by a much more humanistic, caring philosophy and practice. Chapter 6 summarises his conference presentation.

Chapter 5

Japanese Educational Reform: Towards the 21st Century

by

Tomiji Sugawa
Ministry of Education, Science, Sports and Culture, Japan

Schooling in the era of lifelong learning

What direction will Japanese schooling take in the future, particularly with respect to lifelong learning? Technological advancement, internationalisation and changes in the industrial structure are profoundly changing Japanese society and creating the need constantly to acquire new knowledge to cope with new demands of work and daily life. It has therefore become increasingly important to create a "lifelong learning society" where people can freely choose their learning opportunities at any point during their lives and have their achievements recognised. While the true purpose of schooling should be to build a foundation for lifelong learning and to cultivate the basis for personal development, Japanese schools have in fact tended to operate as if they must teach all required knowledge and skills during the school years.

Recently, *Monbusho* conducted an assessment of elementary and lower secondary students' understanding of the contents of the current school curriculum. Students proved to be good at mathematics, reading and comprehension, and knowledgeable in science, history, and geography. However, the assessment criticised the passive nature of learning, as students have neither the opportunity nor motivation sufficiently to think independently and express their own ideas. Other surveys and observations confirm this evaluation.

The vision of schooling as a finite period during which all required knowledge is taught needs to be modified. Instead, schooling must focus on essentials so that children can continue to learn throughout their lifetimes in this era of dramatic change. Particular attention needs to be paid to developing children's capacity to learn independently and to deal with change. Education should be based on a new concept of scholastic ability.

Central Council for Education's report

Education is the basis for all social systems; it is therefore a matter of intense concern to national policy-makers. Japanese educational reform is inseparable from other major reforms in government administration and fiscal and economic structure that the current government is committed to implementing. In January 1997, *Monbusho* defined a Programme for educational reform, and a timetable for its implementation.

Shortly prior to this, the Central Council for Education (CCE), an advisory body to the Education Minister on important aspects of educational policy, produced a report in 1996 proposing three fundamental levels for consideration regarding the future of education. First, education should promote matters that have eternal value such as children's own rich humanity. Second, it should foster children's capacity to deal rapidly with societal changes. Third, it should nurture their vital abilities, or *ikiru-chikara*, in conjunction with schools, families and local communities. These refer to a set of abilities that include, for example, the ability to identify problems, to learn and think independently, to make judgements and to articulate and solve problems more effectively. They also refer to the development of a rich sense of humanity and a healthy body in order to lead a vigorous life. This third aspect is one of the most important concepts in the CCE report.

The report recommends that schools nurture these vital abilities rather than simply transmit knowledge, and that they develop the capacity to teach children to think independently. Schools should do this by producing a rich environment and a more relaxed educational process. Those from countries and cultures with more individualistic perspectives may wonder why Japan has begun to emphasise these kinds of aims and abilities as a matter of policy. The straightforward answer is that contemporary Japanese society needs citizens with these abilities.

More specifically, the report makes recommendations to reduce the burden of school hours, enhance choices, and promote interdisciplinarity and the human side of learning. It recommends that there should be a strict selection of educational content, concentrating on essentials and reducing teaching hours so that children have more time to develop vital abilities. Currently, elementary school students spend between 25-29 hours (each hour defined as 45 minutes long) per week in school while lower secondary school students spend 30 hours (an hour being 50 minutes at the secondary level) and upper secondary school students spend 32 hours in school per week.

Within reduced hours, the CCE recommends that more should be available for elective study in lower secondary schools. Currently, in grade 7, four school hours are allocated for elective study, six in grade 8, and eight school hours in grade 9. Similarly, it argues for the reduction of the number of compulsory subject credits and expansion in the range of electives in upper secondary schools. Currently, compulsory subjects account for about half of graduation credits.

Furthermore, the CCE wants teaching hours to be devoted to interdisciplinary or integrated study to give children a greater opportunity to experience task-based or hands-on learning, to develop international understanding, to deal with an information-oriented society, and environmental understanding. Hands-on experience such as volunteer work, workplace experience, and activity in a natural environment should be promoted as a valuable way to nurture each student's human qualities.

To deal with societal changes, the report offers suggestions for implementing educational reform. Seven of the suggested priorities can be noted here. There is need, the report argues, to:

– Promote international understanding through education.

– Take a systematic approach to learning about information and communications from elementary schools through to upper secondary schools so that children can use information systems and actively disseminate their thoughts and findings.

– Improve the quality of education by creating or making fuller use of communication networks between schools and other institutions. Networks should also be developed to improve learning opportunities in rural areas and for children receiving medical treatment.

– Deal with the pitfalls and problems raised by the information society such as the weakening of human relationships.

– Value each child's unique thinking and experience; the aim here is to cultivate scientific perception and thinking.

– Promote environmental education to develop awareness of these matters.

– Enhance children's understanding of the basic issues raised by an ageing society and increase the opportunities to participate in volunteer work on behalf of senior citizens. Schools should be encouraged to share facilities with nursing homes.

Revising the National Curriculum Guidelines (Courses of Study)

How will these recommendations be realised? Revising the National Curriculum Guidelines is fundamental for this. School education seeks to foster the healthy development of each individual and to do so, and to ensure an optimum national level of education, *Monbusho* lays down Courses of Study for schools throughout Japan. Based on reviews by the Curriculum Council, an advisory body to the Minister of Education, Courses of Study are revised by *Monbusho* every ten years or so.

The current Courses of Study were revised in 1992 and took effect for elementary schools in the same year, for lower secondary schools in 1993, and for upper secondary schools in 1994. The underlying philosophy behind these curricular changes is the

81

promotion of education based on respect for the individual. Educational content and course teaching hours have been addressed in view of the following four aims:

- Fostering human qualities and an awareness of the richness of humanity.

- Emphasising basics and promoting education which encourages individuality: underpinning the current Courses of Study are the basic aspects of education regarded as essential for future citizens, with greater consideration to be given to individuality.

- Fostering a capacity for self-education: priorities set by the Courses of Study include developing children's ability to deal positively with social change as well as their creativity.

- Respect for Japanese culture and traditions and the promotion of international understanding: the current Courses of Study state that fostering respect for Japanese culture and traditions should be a priority, while at the same time enhanced efforts are needed to increase understanding of other national cultures and histories.

In 1996, the Education Minister asked the new Curriculum Council to review the current Courses of Study so that schools might better meet the demands of the 21st century. Following the recommendation from the Central Council for Education, the Curriculum Council is examining the content of schooling, with the view of better instilling vital abilities in children by giving them more time to think. To achieve this, school time should be reorganised into a five-day week. *Monbusho* will revise the Courses of Study on the basis of the council's recommendations.

The five-day school week

One immediate policy concern for Japanese education is the smooth introduction of a five-day school week. A semi-monthly five-day school week was introduced in 1992, giving children and teachers every other Saturday off. Although this five-day school week is popular with children and teachers, many parents have been less positive about it because they believe that children should stay longer at school. Hence, the five-day school week is a controversial subject.

From an educational perspective, the important issue is whether it will help children to develop and to resolve their educational problems. There are at least two main aspects to consider. First, in recent years, various problems have been noted in relation to the character development of Japanese children. These include the lack of experience with activities in a natural environment and in society, the need for an enriching moral education, and poor socialisation because of fewer children per family. Resolving these problems requires rethinking the roles of schools, families and local communities. Second, to raise children who are able to adapt and live independently in a changing society requires education that is inspired by a new vision of scholastic ability – a vision that emphasises the willingness to learn, and the ability to re-think as necessary, judge and express oneself. These qualities cannot be developed in schools alone; the other settings of daily life should reinforce them.

To this end, the full five-day school week should be seen as an opportunity – to re-think education in the light of lives and needs in schools, families and local communities, with a view to developing children with healthy characters and pursuing a new concept of scholastic ability. Given the planned implementation of the full five-day school week, the current Courses of Study will have to be revised to promote such attributes and abilities.

Promoting diversity in upper secondary schools

The achievements of educational reform in upper secondary education deserve particular attention. Japanese upper secondary schools prepare students for advancement to higher education through general courses and for employment through vocational courses. The upper secondary school system has undergone more far-reaching transformation over recent years than either elementary or lower secondary schools due to its rapid expansion and to changing social demands. Fifty years ago, the overall advancement rate to upper secondary school was around 40 per cent; today the rate is 97 per cent. Indeed, the advancement rate to higher and post-secondary education institutions is now well above that to upper secondary education fifty years ago, at over 60 per cent. This expansion of students attending upper secondary schools means they now have a very diverse profile of abilities, interests and concerns.

Over and above overall participation rates, while the percentage of students enrolled in general courses has increased steadily so as now to stand at about 75 per cent, the percentage of students enrolled in vocational courses has correspondingly fallen to 25 per cent. Several problems concerning upper secondary schools have become highlighted. Most general courses are geared towards university entrance examinations, and therefore tend to have uniform curricula. Consequently, they do not provide for the diversity of students' abilities and interests. Another problem is that while approximately 20 per cent of general course graduates enter the workforce upon graduation, yet there is virtually no preparation for employment even at a basic level. More needs to be done to encourage vocational course students to advance to universities if they so wish. It is also clear that vocational course categories have not kept pace with changing industrial structures.

In 1991, the Central Council for Education advised that these problems needed to be addressed through the following broad changes. Efforts should focus on enhancing quality of teaching, programmes, and learning rather than on measures geared to expanding numbers of students and participation rates. Choices should be expanded: the system should be changed to allow students to choose from a wide range of schools, courses and subjects. Competition should be reduced: selection criteria should be diversified to reduce the excessively competitive entrance examinations. Within these broad aims, a number of concrete reforms have been implemented, as described below.

Integrated courses

The integrated course in upper secondary schools was created in 1994 as a third option in addition to the general and vocational courses. Currently, 74 schools offer integrated courses that straddle two other, otherwise separate courses. Such courses enhance the degree of choice available to students to study the subjects that interest them: over 120 subjects are usually offered in an integrated course, compared with about 45 subjects in a general course.

The expectation is that the integrated courses will help students to develop their individual skills to advanced levels, and encourage their willingness and ability to approach tasks actively. Furthermore, integrated courses emphasise the strengthening of students' awareness of careers and their future choices regarding employment. To this end, a new subject called "industrial society and human beings" has been created within the integrated course structure. School guidance has also been expanded to provide advice on subject and career choices.

Credit-based upper secondary schools

The first credit-based upper secondary school was created in 1988. The curriculum is not defined around grades nor is advancement to the next grade dependent on completing a year of study. Students are instead allowed to graduate whenever they have accumulated the required number of credits. The school allows diversity in tailoring upper secondary education to students' needs. Given the greater flexibility this offers to individuals in matching education to their needs and achievements, this is an important development in the light of promoting lifelong learning.

Accreditation of studies at other institutions

To meet the diverse study needs of students, new measures have been introduced for accrediting studies undertaken at schools other than those they normally attend. This may be at upper secondary schools which offer courses otherwise unavailable and at special training or vocational schools; in both cases, the studies are accredited at the student's own school. Credit may also be acquired for success in proficiency tests relating to advanced skills and diverse qualifications. Credits acquired through such means can accumulate up to one quarter of total graduation credits.

These accreditation measures are based on the idea that schools should not confine the areas of students' study within the opportunities available in particular establishments, and that recognizing external achievements is useful for building the foundations for lifelong learning. It is fair to say, however, that these possibilities for wider accreditation have not been fully exploited to date, and more could be done and encouraged. *Monbusho* also intends to expand the scope of accreditation measures to include volunteer work, workplace training and other types of experience.

* * *

These are some of the main directions and proposals for reform present in Japan today. The needs of the 21st century individual and citizen lie firmly at their core. In this presentation I have described one country's reform agenda to foster the school of tomorrow which hopefully provides useful insights and points of comparison with the situation in other countries.

OECD 1999

Chapter 6

The Caring Flexible School for Tomorrow

by

Akira Ninomiya
Hiroshima University, Japan

Introduction

It is very important that we are engaging now in discussions about visions of the 21st century, and the directions and models for schooling for tomorrow that our educational policies should reflect. Schooling should enable youth and adults alike to respond to the rapidly changing societies of today and tomorrow. It must facilitate lifelong learning so as to develop the competences and skills, knowledge and understanding, attitudes and minds required for the next century. Future schools must prepare children to think creatively and critically, and they must motivate them to define and resolve emerging problems. The curriculum will need to be innovative and the teaching process improved to meet these challenges.

To realise these different aims, information and communication technology (ICT) should be actively and critically utilised, with particular attention given to extending learning opportunities for all through these means. Those who can access knowledge and information through technology and those who cannot are coming to occupy very different, unequal grounds; already, possession of information literacy and technology capital differentiates populations and nations. Despite the promise of technology to bridge the learning limitations imposed by time and space, the gap between those who can and cannot access information continues to grow. Inequality of opportunity, recast in the light of these new dimensions of information access and ICT, needs to be addressed with the same priority that access to different educational provision/cycles received in many countries in the 1960s and 1970s.

The caring school environment

The nature of schooling needs to be redefined if it is to be appropriate for the world of the 21st century as outlined above. In the process of modernisation to now, there has been a tendency to emphasise the nature of teaching and training required for basic knowledge and skills. Children are socialised into cultural assumptions about "more" and "efficiency": quicker is regarded as better, more efficient has become synonymous with more effective learning. Yet, we know that modern schooling has come in for critical scrutiny. Educators, parents, experts and educational policy leaders are examining different options and innovative approaches, *inter alia* home schooling, charter schools, virtual or digital schooling. These all demonstrate a certain dissatisfaction with existing provision as people search for something different for their children and for themselves. An understanding of why this is the case and what they want should inform future policy developments.

I have my own particular vision of what schooling should be about. Schooling for tomorrow should be marked by a shift from a preoccupation with training and control and with selecting the young, to caring for them and their future. In my view, caring is the most important of the school's functions. Students should always know that someone cares for them – their future, their inner life, their hopes, dreams, and problems, their family, friends, and career. "I" becomes the central character in the schooling process. Each student should be able to feel that someone – a teacher or another adult in the school – is always looking out for "me". "I" can feel better about being in school, and can arrive there happily each morning. "I" ought to feel that schooling is for "me". Later, each student should be able to recall schooldays with affection and good memories, especially for the people who did so care for "me".

This is a vision of the school culture and system with implications for curriculum, student guidance, discipline, for openness to the community and to other resources, pupil-teacher relationships and more. We should replace the discouraging school environment that is all too prevalent today. Schooling for tomorrow should engender a sense of pride and a positive self-image. It should be personalised and individualised, and made more flexible through the extensive use of multi-media and ICT. There should be global and local community involvement, new and innovative pedagogy.

Comparing this vision with current arrangements, including in the Japanese system, suggests important changes. "Choice" and "caring" should become the key words for schooling for tomorrow. The nature and climate of schooling should be such that bullying, suicide and other serious suffering have no place. Through such change, schools for tomorrow will be more able to prepare children and others for the newly emerging skills and competences required for the 21st century. Positive experiences and memories of being cared for can help us learn to live together and become motivated through a sense of empowerment to face the difficult global and local challenges that we now confront.

Schooling beyond time and space

The second main aspect I would identify to characterise schooling for tomorrow would be that it should move beyond the restrictions of time and space. Now, for the most part, classes are provided from early morning to the afternoon, within the fixed locations of school buildings; education is limited within these space and time boundaries. Schools' social systems and values have been developed and "purified" through the long, careful efforts of the educational authorities and teachers. Instructional materials have also been carefully developed to meet different didactical and pedagogical needs. Pupils study the textbooks and the knowledge they contain within packaged time periods. Teachers impart the accepted, authorised knowledge. In sum, the learning that takes place within our specialised school buildings has been carefully developed, manipulated and purified to meet the aims of school education.

This is not a haphazard process, nor without profound consequences. Especially in non-European countries, modern schooling has been one of the most important means of putting in place the knowledge and skills necessary for nation-building. Especially since World War II, schooling in Japan has played a very important role in teaching unfamiliar and non-traditional knowledge, and the new values of "democracy". These did not emerge from the earlier history of the people, nor through institutions in the community and families. Instead, they were transported into the society with schools as the main vehicle. Schooling has required such extensive investments of time precisely because the instruction has been in knowledge and skills that were otherwise unfamiliar. No wonder that pupils had to come to school early in the morning and spend long hours in the classroom!

From now on, the main aims of schooling should not be about the transmission of what had been unfamiliar knowledge and skills. What should be taught instead are the new literacies and skills for the identification and solving of problems, creative and critical thinking, self-motivated and self-directed learning with a view to laying the foundation of a lifetime as a learner. As schooling moves into a new generation, it should become the place where students can challenge and think creatively and independently in ways that connect strongly to real life society. It should cease to be the place where pupils memorise and learn by heart packaged "school knowledge" through purified textbooks and curricula. The new goals of schooling thus call for fundamental innovations and change in the dominant concept of education.

I foresee this new generation of schooling as providing far greater learning opportunities derived from the real world of the surrounding society and community. People will come into school from the community, bringing with them their ideas and experiences. In some cases, they might even bring advanced expertise, such as new high-technologies from researchers in laboratories (*e.g.* in communications, bio-science, or engineering) or from the universities and colleges. ICT can be used more efficiently and educationally to move beyond the physical constraints of the school buildings to promote new forms of teaching and learning drawing on real-life materials and community expertise. Students ought to learn about the issues that exercise their fathers, mothers, brothers and sisters, and others in the community and society. Environmental learning is an area *par excellence* where students can learn from the realities outside school. Textbooks and other learning materials should also be changed; a small but significant step in this direction would be to replace the illustrations in textbooks by real pictures. It is not just a matter of who comes into school but also that students should go out into the community and let these "external" influence shape their values, knowledge and skills.

ICT can underpin the new learning environments to promote self-motivated and self-directed learning. The traditional library should be transformed into a "media centre", giving pupils access to knowledge databases through computers, where they can surf for targeted knowledge in an open way and seek solutions to their learning problems and tasks. Students and teachers would be able to stay at the media centre in the school building or at home and from there access databases, the National Library in Tokyo, a specialised institution in the United States or wherever. Teachers would not need to prepare pre-structured class instructions but would facilitate the pupils to find ways of solving learning tasks and problems. They can and should help the students to understand that there is a multitude of ways to solve problems, and that there is often a variety of solutions.

Traditional class-instruction scheduling will need to change for the new learning environment using hyper-media and the Internet. Pupils might instead sit at the computer display in the morning to find their own study tasks on that day, which have been planned and co-ordinated with the teachers as facilitators. Then they might request the information resources needed through the learning material and resource staff using e-mail or seek the material in the Internet home pages through search engines. They would be strongly discouraged from printing these out on paper (which so often is then simply put to one side), but asked to read the screened pages and take notes directly. Even if the material is derived from the Internet, it should not just become an alternative textbook in which pupils will lose interest.

Having spent some hours to find information, and some more to solve set problems and learning tasks, students may sometimes then write papers or produce models or some other outcome, perhaps collaboratively with others. They may then send their work to teachers who are either present in the classroom or elsewhere but contactable *via* e-mail. The teachers may ask for more work to be completed, or for students to engage collaboratively with other schools, even with other countries, through the networking of schools on the Internet. As that is completed, the next tasks might then involve the teacher providing conventional instruction. Or instead, students might work on small group activities. The important point is not how much the teachers teach but how much and how the pupils learn, in and outside the schools, with flexible and individualised scheduling. The delineation of learning tasks might resemble a form of contract. Performance should be monitored so that each pupil has the most relevant and appropriate learning tasks for them.

This does away with conventional notions of time and scheduling that suppose that every pupil can and should learn the same knowledge and skills within the set instructional period. Pupils should be able to plan their own schedules of learning in and outside the schools, whether relating to the academic year or term, the month, the week or the day. The school should direct them to what is strongly recommended to learn in the school curriculum and help students to learn through facilitating learning tasks, problem-solving, etc., as described earlier. This philosophy of learning and studying would be the ethos of the new generation of schools.

The increasing gap among the pupils: old and new stories

The third main aspect of schooling in the 21st century to be addressed are the many negative consequences that arise from the gap between the families that are information-rich and the information-poor, the education-friendly and the education-indifferent, the technologically-equipped and the non-equipped. Cultural and information capitals make so much of the learning difference between students, regions, and countries. These differences become wider and more telling in the context of rapid change in technology innovation, globalisation and internationalisation. I expect these gaps to continue to widen. Can we prevent such new inequality of the outcomes and performances of the pupils caused by their total learning environments? Can a revamped notion of compensatory education help to create fair competition among the pupils? Unfortunately, experience to date does not suggest very optimistic answers to these questions.

So, from the equity and social policy viewpoints, schools are crucial institutions and the policy questions perplexing and important. Does the school enhance equality of quality education or instead increase the gap among pupils that result from differing family backgrounds? At the end of the 20th century, equality of schooling has been improved and this has been a major aim of policy. In the beginning of 21st century, will it continue to be a major policy aim? In order at least to maintain the present level of learning equality, given the impact of the globalisation and information technology revolutions, more money is likely to be needed for educational investment. The costs of investing in technology and global networking are higher than we had expected. But this is not all, for the costs involved in maintaining equality of quality education as regards communication skills, information literacy, and high motivation for dealing with uncertainty are also likely to be high. Are governments willing to spend more money on education in the next century? At least while there is enthusiasm to privatise schooling, the signs are that this willingness is still lacking.

Conclusions

It will be clear to the reader that I believe that there must be approaches towards the definition of schooling that depart from traditional models and that can become reality. One of the case studies of innovative schooling in Japan is a Junior High School in Tokyo where the school building and a facility for the elderly are on the same campus. The young and old share the location and work together, so that the school prepares the students to live with the elderly in today's ageing society. This is one important function of schooling for tomorrow: to help young people to live together and to provide the opportunity for them to understand those of other generations. Another innovative national case is the elementary school where the community is invited in to teach the children at school. The example of partnership between schools and the community in this way will also be commonplace in schooling for tomorrow. In Japan, too, we have the Internet network of schools called the One Hundred Schools project; a private communications company has developed the school network Comet, whereby the schools are increasingly woven together through the interconnections of the Internet. These technologically interlinked examples are also models for schooling for tomorrow.

In the 21st century, schooling will change drastically: its curriculum, the teachers, the school management, etc. Schooling for tomorrow will expand its roles and responsibilities. No matter how the schooling for tomorrow will meet the emerging demands, I hope – I assume – that tomorrow's schools will be better than those of today.

Rapporteur's Conclusions

by

Donald Hirsch
Education Policy Consultant, Guildford, United Kingdom

Donald Hirsch's work as rapporteur began well before participants gathered at Hiroshima University. He orchestrated an electronic discussion group that continued up to the linked "virtual" seminar that took place alongside the "face-to-face" debate in Japan. He has incorporated the "virtual seminar" into these conclusions and has used quotations emerging from that source. He has reflected the comments, debates, and working group discussions and conclusions, as well as the papers that provide the basis of the foregoing chapters. The chapter is the rapporteur's conclusions, not a synthesis of papers, reflecting his choice of the key ideas and arguments from among the very rich discussions that took place.

* * *

"In Hiroshima, we always feel responsible to future generations." Dr. Kazuhiro Mori, Vice-president, University of Hiroshima.

Eighty people from 25 countries, meeting in person and *via* e-mail, were in broad agreement: our schools will need to be different tomorrow if they are to cater for tomorrow's needs. This seminar brought together a wide variety of policy-makers, academics, teachers and others. All shared a belief that new approaches to schooling are required if the school as an institution is to flourish, in societies in which the pursuit of knowledge has become transformed in character and significance. Many brought visions of the kind of innovation that is needed; some brought examples of how new technologies, pedagogical or organisational tools can bring about worthwhile change.

Yet they also shared a sense that education systems are highly resistant to fundamental changes in the way in which schooling is conducted. True innovation, it was felt, had not yet acquired a political legitimacy or a public acceptance, partly because it appeared to cut across traditional and deeply held convictions about what education should be for. There was a spectrum of optimism/pessimism about the prospects for spreading innovation. But an important, radical message to all schools was "adapt or decline". In a world in which knowledge flows more plentifully and openly than ever before, schools that do not address what is important to young people could have a waning influence on what and how they learn.

This seminar was a first step in CERI's response to an invitation to the OECD, by Ministers of Education, to "study promising approaches, identify examples of good practice for wider dissemination (...)", and "(...) assess alternative visions of the 'school of tomorrow', in particular in the light of new technologies and advances in pedagogy". As well as assembling some interesting first examples of these approaches and visions, the seminar sent back a strong message that the development of promising models would not in itself create change. For schooling systems as a whole to start to operate differently was a far greater challenge.

In confronting this challenge, schools and education systems will need to construct new approaches without wholly dismantling established ones. It is particularly important to retain confidence of parents and the public, and not to take schools too rapidly down dark, unexplored avenues. The main part of this chapter summarises the discussion about tomorrow's schools in terms of four ways in which established strengths of schools can be adapted and new ones developed. First it looks at how the objectives for schooling need to be adapted. Second, it looks at the development of new relationships in the process of schooling, which were seen at the seminar as a major aspect of change. Third, it looks at how views of the content of schooling are being broadened. Finally, it looks at how the infrastructure of schooling might be adapted in order to address more effectively the desired objectives, to develop the desired relationships and to deliver the desired content.

Adapting the objectives of the school

"The collective appropriation from parents of the right to educate children is one of the most unquestioned tasks of the state. But for how long?" Walo Hutmacher, University of Geneva.

"Innovation is accomplished when not only new procedures but also new objectives or aims are established, for example: 'developing one's abilities in full', creating self-confidence, creativeness, democratic values, the use of a scientific method, critical capacity." Arsenio Inclán, Colegio Liceo Europeo, Madrid.

The idea of educating a rounded individual capable of critical thought was not invented with the information age. But, especially in cultures that have developed a relatively didactic style of teaching, there is now both a pressure and an opportunity for a radical change of emphasis in schooling.

The pressure comes from the changing world. The emergence of so-called "knowledge-oriented societies" has made it important for everybody to acquire not just a wide range of subject knowledge but new skills and competences that make them adaptable problem-solvers and self-motivated learners, capable of facing unpredictable challenges throughout the life-cycle. Some of the biggest changes arise from the transformation of work (where there is less demand for unskilled or repetitive activity) and of employment (which offers fewer stable, supportive structures). Closely linked to economic change is a new social context, which puts schools in the position of educating young people with fewer stable reference-points and much less certainty about their futures. At the same time, a panoply of alternative new influences compete to shape young people's lives, not always in directions that society considers healthy or desirable. The opening up of information through global communications technologies is likely to increase the power of such influences over young people, in competition to familiar sources of knowledge and information including schools.

Some fear that a multiplicity of information sources and social pressures will cause societies to fragment, and would like to see revitalised schools as providing some of the missing "social glue". There is potentially a contradiction between this social function and the potential for schools to support highly individualised models of study based around individual students retrieving information and developing their own learning pathways. But the seminar working group on the social dimension formulated a vision of the school as "a competent co-ordinator and facilitator of learning, cultural and social activities in learning communities". This ambitious objective requires a big change in mind-set from that which sees the school mainly as a transmitter of knowledge, behind closed doors, to a group of young people. One of the strongest features of the innovative schools represented at the seminar was the high degree of partnership with parents and with their surrounding communities, on more equal terms than had hitherto been the case.

The opportunity to meet new challenges comes partly from technology, but also from the very changes in the social structures that are creating the pressures. Communities often look to the unifying power of schools in support of their desire to reinvent themselves. The willingness and in some cases insistence of parents to be more involved in the schooling of their children is growing fast. As expressed in Professor Hutmacher's words quoted at the beginning of this section, parents may lose patience with educators unless there is better collaboration between the home and the school. A familiar argument is that this arises because parents are on average more educated and assertive as consumers than in the past.

A newer argument is that knowledge and learning tools are becoming so easily available through the Internet and other sources that educated parents could start to see a diminishing need for schooling itself. Professors David Hargreaves and Kerry Kennedy, two of the lead experts at the seminar, expressed visions of the future in which alternative access to knowledge and learning could become so strong that educated parents who are disenchanted with schools rely increasingly on some form of home schooling. Many were alarmed by this scenario – fearing that learning would depend even more than at present on one's family's cultural capital, and that socially and culturally unifying functions of schools would be eroded.　　95

Professor Hargreaves was less pessimistic, envisaging the development of new hybrids between learning in homes, schools and elsewhere, and suggesting that the threat of flight could act as an incentive for schools to innovate (if they are allowed to develop distinctive missions) and to co-operate more with parents.

So, there are plenty of reasons for schools to adopt new objectives, especially in terms of the skills that they develop in children and the partnerships that they develop with communities. But a complicating factor is that the pressure is to add these objectives to existing ones, rather than replacing them. There remain strong political and public pressures to retain a traditional concept of what is to be learned in school subjects; parents in particular want to be sure that their children are learning "the basics". There is no necessary contradiction between old desires for example to ensure that children become literate and numerate, and a new stress on nurturing children's capacity to use such skills flexibly and creatively. However, and particularly in countries that make a rise in educational standards a priority, there is pressure for familiar forms of testing to demonstrate that satisfactory standards have been reached. As discussed further below, innovators have not sufficiently been able to demonstrate in these terms that their projects meet old as well as new educational objectives. So there remains a tension between the two. Part of the aim of partnerships between schools and parents must be to develop closer understandings that start to resolve that tension.

Developing new relationships

"Successful businesses have to create knowledge. Schools too need to create rather than just transmit knowledge." David Hargreaves, University of Cambridge.

From the "virtual" seminar: *"We know how living systems work on principles of interdependence, diversity, cycling and recycling, energy flow, sustainability and carrying capacity, etc. Schools need to become living systems, not machines, factories or boxes that create mechanical students and approaches to learning."* Carole Cooper, Global Learning Communities International.

Partnerships between schools and those outside depend on much more than communication and contact. The seminar explored a series of new relationships between teachers, children, parents and others in the community. These raised the issue of the relationships between all these actors and knowledge.

At the centre of the discussion was the proposition that education should no longer revolve around the transmission of knowledge from teacher to student. Various new roles could be developed including:

– Teachers as producers of knowledge. For schools to become learning organisations, teachers need to develop their own expertise as well as helping students to access the expertise of others. The potential for them to participate in the creation of knowledge (including professional know-how) has grown, through the opportunities for collaborative networks offered by new forms of electronic communication. The construction of such networks depends not just on technological possibilities but on the way humans interact. Many of the innovative examples referred to at the seminar involved greater interaction both within and among schools, by teachers who had previously been isolated in their classrooms. A number of participants in the "virtual" seminar pointed out that in the case of collaborative curricular projects involving the Internet, technology could stimulate contacts which, even though they might always have been possible, had not hitherto occurred.

– Students as producers of knowledge. The idea that students too might collaborate, across the world, to develop their own knowledge rather than just receiving wisdom from their teachers, was seen as highly attractive in principle. In practice, inspiring examples included the "Twenty-first Century Schoolhouse", which brings together high school students in six countries in an ambitious exercise to develop a new international environmental agenda, drawing on projects distinctive to the geography of each of their countries.

– Schools, parents and communities as co-learners. The multiplying of learning resources that are not necessarily channelled through academic networks makes it possible for knowledge to be spread and developed in many different directions. Much contact with parents continues to be on a highly unequal footing in this respect: it can consist of schools informing parents of what they are doing, rather than developing a mission jointly with them. This does not mean that schools should play down their own expertise, but they should also recognise what others can contribute. There was considerable discussion for example of the role of non-teachers in schools. A number of case studies illustrated how their expertise could be called on provided that arrangements for the use of different kinds of personnel are sufficiently flexible.

An important aspect that was stressed about these features of change is that they should be treated as a whole rather than parts of separate policies. One of the problems with initiatives coming from central governments (which did not enjoy great popularity among the seminar's innovators) is that they tend to be disjointed, tackling one problem at a time. But the living or "organic" character of learning organisations implies an integrated strategy for change.

The enthusiasm of participants in Hiroshima for students organising their own learning brought two contrasting responses from the seminar's remote participants:

"There is a limit to having students become producers of knowledge. Valuable as this might be for the development of students and the production of knowledge, it depends on the careful

guidance of a knowledgeable teacher who will ensure that students do not 'lose their way'." Bruce Sheppard, Memorial University of Newfoundland.

"There are no limits to students as producers of knowledge. The limits come in the strictures we as teachers impose on them – either from our lack of experience, our fears, or our lack of appreciation of what they have to offer us as learners." Julie Boyd, Global Learning Communities International.

Although these statements are not necessarily as contradictory as they may first appear, the task of redefining the role of the teacher is not easy. There is a general consensus that teachers should be facilitators or mediators of knowledge, but that this should not be their only role. Most importantly, they should continue to provide students with a sense of direction. They may not be able to master all information in their subject areas, but they should continue to be experts in knowledge and in the development of knowledge-related skills.

As the sources of knowledge become more diffuse and its flow more bewildering, the traditional role of teacher as guide and mentor is if anything reasserted. The difference of emphasis in the comments quoted above, however, illustrates how difficult it can be to apply this principle in practice. What for one person is firm guidance might for another be undue constraint of youthful inquisitiveness. The balance that is found within schools and classrooms is likely to vary considerably from one culture to another. In particular, the degree to which teachers and children are able to explore their own learning avenues will depend on the degree to which central control over content is maintained. This is the subject of the following section.

Redefining the content

"The school curriculum needs to be used to create sense of community and common values (…). Is there a role for the curriculum in a world with no boundaries to knowledge acquisition? (…) How do we avoid overprescription on the one hand, and fragmentation on the other?" Kerry Kennedy, University of Canberra.

"The characteristic and ability most called for in the future world is zest for living to cope with an acutely changing society: the ability to identify problems for oneself, learn by oneself, think for oneself, make independent judgements and actions and solve problems (…). A rich sense of humanity capable of self-reliance, co-operation with others, compassion for others and sensitivity to feeling (…)." Central Council for Education, Japan.

Japan's Education Ministry is moving towards a five-day week for schools, in order to slim down the subject content of the curriculum and put greater emphasis on children's experience outside formal education. Its decision to reduce progressively Saturday attendance of school is popular with teachers and with pupils, but less so with parents, many of whom themselves have to work a six-day week.

The Japanese concept of schools teaching a "rich sense of humanity" enjoyed considerable support at the seminar. Yet, the widely expressed objective of moving from an excessively subject-laden curriculum, towards one that emphasises skills, values and character, is unevenly applied, because of conflicting pressures. As the Japanese example shows, much may depend on one's starting-point. In East Asian countries where the value of hard work has traditionally been strong, there has recently been increasing concern to place relatively more stress on characteristics such as initiative and inventiveness. Malaysia has recently introduced a subject called "invention" into 100 schools. Whether such subjects can be systematically taught, let alone introduced by government decree, remains to be determined. It appeared from the seminar that Asian innovators are more inclined than Western ones to talk more specifically about the skills and knowledge that will be needed by children in the next century, whereas Western ones often focus more on teaching and learning processes, leaving considerable autonomy in the hands of schools and communities. However, centrally-driven reform efforts in countries such as the United Kingdom and the United States have tried to put more stress than in the past on measures to achieve higher standards in basic subjects such as mathematics and science, in which East Asian countries do so well relative to others on international tests.

One key issue taken up by the seminar's curriculum working group was the apparent difficulty in orienting teaching more around "learning skills" such as problem-solving, researching and thinking. Although governments say they want students to "learn to learn", schools tend to be very poor at imparting these skills. It is hard to deliver such change through curriculum specifications, and the problem is rather to create the right conditions in schools and classrooms.

An underlying question for any type of curriculum change is therefore how far governments ought to continue to determine the agenda. A widely held view was that governments have much less power to promote cultural identity through a curriculum than they used to have, because of the unstoppable force of global communication. Moreover, if true innovation, for example in teaching practices, derives from the bottom up, government control is more likely to get in the way of genuine school improvement rather than promote it. Professor Kennedy formulated the maxim that governments should therefore move from control to leadership. This does not imply complete autonomy for schools, and governments have a legitimate interest in pursuing fundamental equity issues, to ensure that all children have access to a demanding set of knowledge and skills. In some cases, governments have used a common curriculum as the main tool for this purpose.

In most countries, the government is a long way from relinquishing control over the levers that set the curriculum groundrules under which schools must operate. Even where it is modest in defining what will be studied and when, its influence on assessment can limit the advisability of departing too far from recognised norms. In this context, there is an uneasy relationship between the old and the new. If knowledge is manifested in many new ways, but tested only in old ones, all the incentives are for "safe" strategies rather than for risk-taking.

99

A new learning infrastructure?

"The Internet has allowed for a redefinition of the classroom, the role of the teacher, the role of the learner, and the nature of knowledge (...). Not only does the learning process involve acquiring knowledge and digesting it, but also producing knowledge for other to acquire and digest. The learner becomes active for all the world to see." David Lloyd, Webmaster, Twenty-first Century Schoolhouse Project.

A new infrastructure for learning can support powerful techniques for realising the new objectives, relationships and content of schooling that have been referred to above. This is too wide a subject to cover comprehensively, but three particular aspects of the learning infrastructure were particularly relevant to the Hiroshima discussion: the organisation of the school, the use of technology, and the physical and temporal organisation of instruction. The degree to which these features have transformed varies – from quite a bit in the case of the first, to hardly at all in the case of the last.

The independent and assertive outlook of innovative schools from a wide range of countries was itself symptomatic of a fundamental change that is taking place in school organisation. Devolution of decisions and organisational authority to school level is a near universal trend. The degree of autonomy varies considerably across countries, however, as does the definition of which aspects of schooling are locally controlled. Part of the frustration of schools in some countries is that while budgets and management are increasingly devolved, decisions over content are increasingly centralised. This is especially true in some English-speaking countries where there had hitherto been relatively great local freedom over curriculum. But in certain other cases, schools that have hitherto been governed as part of a managed system are starting to be stimulated by a new freedom in taking a wide area of decision-making. An optimistic scenario for the future is that as this devolution progresses, great innovative energies will be released.

A second aspect of infrastructure, and the one that was most fully discussed at the seminar, was technology. A working group on this theme concluded that whereas new information and communication technologies have been successfully used to meet particular needs – including distance learning in sparsely populated areas, teaching people with physical disabilities and disseminating minority subjects – their use was not yet well integrated into conventional teaching. One important problem was extending and sustaining the efforts of inspired individuals.

In order to encourage the system as a whole to use technology more thoroughly, it would be helpful to demonstrate more systematically the improved learning results and the potential economies that technology could bring. Little evidence of either could be produced. This discussion identified an underlying problem. The objective of the inspired pioneers of these technologies was not to produce the same type of outcome as conventional teaching for less money or at higher levels. A high school student who learns how to write an effective research report on the environment by collecting evidence with peers in half a dozen countries may neither cost less to teach nor perform higher on a curriculum test.

A third element of infrastructure is the one most taken for granted and probably the hardest to change. Is the old model of one-teacher classrooms, with children of the same age taking a series of single-subject lessons necessarily the best way to organise instruction? The case studies brought interesting examples of new departures, in terms of team teaching, interdisciplinary curricula approaches and multi-age classrooms. One interesting classroom model was that of "teaching laboratories" that could be used by some 60 children simultaneously (for example at Warnbro Community School, Western Australia). But these innovations remain at the margins of their systems: the overwhelming model remains the traditional one. This aspect of the infrastructure is bound to be strongly influenced by centrally mandated content and assessment procedures. Multi-disciplinary or open classroom work can be risky if the assessed curriculum is based around well-defined single subject areas. Moreover, parents and the public in many countries are wary of such change, partly because past experiments in more open learning may have confused openness with a lack of rigour and probably underemphasised teacher support.

Conclusion: why reform is not innovation

"Experimental education is not acceptable to the general mass of people (...). It seems that innovation is regarded as experimental and once the experimental tag is applied it can produce many problems." Terry Sanbrook, Warnbro Community School, Western Australia.

After two days pondering the tension between bottom-up innovation and top-down forms of control, the seminar concluded with a revealing discussion of the distinction between innovation and reform. It was suggested that the recent "school reform" movement that had been particularly strong in English-speaking countries had not managed to address the fundamental issue of how to create new models of schooling. In a caricature that was perhaps exaggerated but also contained some truth, one participant described how his country was now superb at testing what young people know but had not worked out how to get them to learn more.

One response to such a dichotomy is simply to tell governments to get out of the way: to create conditions that permit innovation rather than trying to dictate the education agenda. But on reflection, there was an acceptance that government-supported reform and locally-generated innovation need to be seen as complementary rather than opposed to each other. If governments devolve all decisions to schools, some may be inspired to change fundamentally, but the majority may simply go on doing the familiar. So leadership is needed from the centre. But only if teachers can engage with reform, suggested Professor Kennedy, can it be translated into innovation.

It is easy to say that governments should be leaders rather than directors of change, but rather harder to agree on exactly how firmly they should guide schools in matters such as curriculum development. For many of the innovators at the seminar, whose schools found dynamism from within, the answer was hardly at all. But how can such efforts be spread? One helpful model is Portugal's "Good Hope" programme, under which the Ministry of Education wants to exploit good practice without using a top-down approach to spread it. In a strategy aiming to ensure that the spirit of innovation is not lost in its dissemination, the programme collaborates with schools, making interesting cases more visible, and encouraging each school to interpret the lessons in its own way. The programme focuses on examples of successful learning, positive learning environments and on good school management. It offers schools research evidence on what made changes elsewhere work and some resources to support projects. Yet as with so many interesting initiatives, there is a question over how well it will be sustained once the initial term of the programme is completed.

The effective combining of reform and innovation is a difficult challenge. Its success is likely to depend in particular on:

- The development of a good relationship between central and local actors. This requires a mutual tolerance: governments recognising that they cannot control everything, and teachers acknowledging that some areas of action may be constrained by externally defined priorities.

- An effective mixing of what is best of the old and of the new. If the world is divided into revolutionaries and conservatives, there is little prospect for change that is sustainable, rather than being reversed when the next fashion appears.

- An emphasis by innovators on change that is susceptible to evaluation and whose demonstrable benefits therefore make it publicly acceptable. This criterion may make cause some of the more radical ideas for change hard to implement. But it was stressed that exciting innovation is unlikely to make much progress at a system level unless it can be sold as tested improvement.

- Leadership from the middle. The theory of organisations suggests that success comes not from pure "bottom up" or "top down" change but from "middle-up-down" – requiring a middle layer of management to lead as intermediaries between the realities at the bottom and the priorities at the top. Applying this principle to education, it was uncertain whether the "middle" would be school principals or perhaps heads of department. But it is evident that only if school managers work well both with those outside the school and with teachers can a common sense of educational purpose be developed.

So, while 80 people from 25 countries agreed that our schools ought to be different tomorrow if they are to cater for tomorrow's needs, by no means all of them regarded it as inevitable that the desired change would take place. Professor Hutmacher pointed out that every day, schools achieve a startling feat by getting millions of children to assemble at a specified place and time – this very fact is a powerful constant. It may not be enough to create the schools that we want for tomorrow. But true, sustainable change in schooling will only take place as the result of a common will from many quarters, that includes parents and politicians as well as inspired local educators. This seminar demonstrated the importance of building consensus around a common agenda.

Appendix

International Examples of Innovative Schools: a Synthesis

by

OECD Secretariat

In preparation for the Hiroshima seminar, a detailed request for the preparation of country cases was circulated as a common grid. Eighteen countries prepared such notes, describing over 30 examples of innovative schools, initiatives or networks. Many of the seminar participants were those directly involved in the cases. This Appendix brings together a selection of the key features described in these case reports, and the themes they raise. It seeks to maintain the richness of the particular examples. To this end, as much of the original material as possible has been reproduced in its original form.

The broad specification for the selection of the cases was that they should be both innovative and exemplary individual schools or school networks, and represent possible models for consideration as "schools for tomorrow". They might be models driven by "internal" change, through moving towards becoming learning organisations. Or, they might be categorised more as "external" models of innovation through having recast their relationships with their different communities. In addition to such dimensions as background and main characteristics, the cases were asked to refer to evaluation and the results so generated, relevance and generalisability to other schools, and the extent to which the cases have been developed primarily through local action or else as part of a broader drive for change through national reform.

Introduction

The country cases of "schools for tomorrow", while adhering to a common set of criteria for selection, cover a very wide range of aims, practice, and social location. Insofar as they are exemplary for future development, they do not suggest a single model but many. Moreover, in some cases, the country examples were not based on single institutions but networks or movements that embrace some or many schools. Such examples serve as a reminder that to identify "the school" of the future is not necessarily to describe a single institution, with a particular location, personnel and immediate community, and indeed some of the most promising models may not be single schools at all.

While diverse, the cases have not explored the full range of possibilities that schooling might take. No examples of such highly de-institutionalised examples as "home schooling" as referred to by Kennedy, Hargreaves and Ninomiya in their chapters, are included. And, while many of the country examples are schools that have made information and communication technology (ICT) central to their operations (*e.g.* the "global classroom", "the electronic school"), they are still institutions with school walls, teachers, and face-to-face contacts between teachers, students, and parents rather than more "virtual" arrangements. In short, there is no pretence that all the possible models for schooling in the 21st century are comprehensively explored through the country cases. In any case, Hutmacher's discussion of the "constants" of schooling suggests that it is far easier to design novel technical and organisational models for learning than it is to devise arrangements that meet the profound, highly diverse social functions that schools perform, still more to devise these on a society-wide rather than small-scale basis.

There were, such caveats notwithstanding, a wide range of experiences and types of school reported by the countries; this Appendix seeks to reflect their richness through extracts from the cases illustrative of a number of key themes. It is quite another matter to ask how relevant or generalisable such examples are in countries and contexts other than those that generated them. Generalisability is always limited by national culture and context – a school model that works well in Austria, for instance, may not take root in Australia and *vice versa*. The very process of innovation, as discussed by Cros and Hargreaves, rests in dynamic inter-relationship with broader change, and cannot simply be imposed by fiat *via* large-scale reform. There is a further limitation to generalisability: as described in conclusion below, many (but not all) of the country examples were schools in comparatively affluent surrounding, enjoying high levels of parental support, including financial backing, and enviable facilities.

Key aims and outcomes

Several of the main aims outlined in the above chapters recur in these schools. For instance, the emphasis placed by Ninomiya on the school as a "caring environment", and by Kennedy on the importance of social and ethical education, finds an echo in a number of the selected schools. Certain of these are small establishments, perhaps with an "alternative" approach and status, but others are larger mainstream institutions. Even recognising that there may be an important gap between declared aims and actual practice throughout a school, the emphasis on nurture and caring is a feature of several of the cases chosen by countries as representing models of "schools of tomorrow", *e.g.*:

> *The basic principle of Irmak is summarised as "education starts with love and respect for child".* [Irmak, Turkey.]

> *Harumi Junior High School is a unique public school in terms of its facility and educational activities: that is, it is built on the same campus that the Special Facility for the Aged People in Chuo-ku in Tokyo. The unique concept of this school is "schools that live together with the senior people", in the age of ageing society. The emphasis is placed on the concept of "care" and education for welfare.* [Harumi Junior High School, Japan.]

> *The Yungsan Sung-Jee School is (...) very humane and democratic. The school is very small and the teachers have strong commitment to teaching and caring their students (...). All the matters including the curricula are discussed in the general meeting of the school members, students as well as teachers. The students are not forced to be present at the classes. If they feel they are not ready, they are allowed to do what they are interested in. Especially they are encouraged to do work in the farm which the school operates.* [Yungsan Sung-Jee School for Students At-risk, Korea.]

> *The basic approach is to develop the multi-dimensional growth of the individual and to render him/her functional in a world which is undergoing a rapid and dramatic change. This goal is achieved by educating students who are primarily in harmony with themselves and with their environment; who are tolerant; who are respectful of others ideas and beliefs; who are against all violence; who are imbued with humanistic, democratic, national and universal values; who are productive, creative and scientific thinkers; who are inquisitive and meticulous; who are independent achievers; who are able to assume the responsibility of their own decisions; who are adept at expressing themselves; who are self-confident; and, who are ready to take their place in society as independent and free individuals.* [MEF Schools, Istanbul, Turkey.]

Parallel to these expressions of the dominant aims and philiphies underpinning these national examples of "schools of tomorrow" were outcomes suggesting that the prized results were not only, and perhaps not mainly, enhanced examination passes or test score achievements. Many of the schools themselves reported among their key achievements to be improvements in motivation, climate, and inclusion that may translate only indirectly into improved measured results:

> *One of the school's major achievements is that, as a result of this approach, the number of referrals to special education has dropped drastically, in spite of the language problems of many pupils.* [Primary School De Notenkraker, Rotterdam, the Netherlands.]

> *They developed their heart and mind through those programmes. Especially the violence and vandalism were solved easily, since the communication and exchange programmes were developed. Students became very soft, nice and friendly. They developed the attitude of being open. Since the development of the programme, the school became very clean. No graffiti on the wall. No litter on the corridor. No window is broken. No student smokes.* [Harumi Junior High School, Japan.]

At the start of the school-year some students were very individualised and insecure, but as time went by a positive learning environment was established, which among other things has as a result that no one from this class dropped out of school in contrast to the other first-year classes. Some of the quiet and insecure girls had even acquired a self-confidence which enabled them to do better that expected at the oral exams. [Viborg Upper Secondary School, Denmark.]

The number of pupils that are referred to special education is remarkably low: one or (in exceptional cases) two per year, while the average number of referrals in Apeldoorn is 4.8. The scores on national assessment tests are average. [Apeldoorn Primary School, the Netherlands.]

Several schools reported that, however much stress they place on improving motivation through enhancing the learning environment, that this is not in contrast to the conventional aims of improving cognitive learning and achievement levels but frequently as an important means to reach these ends, and in one or two cases this was expressed in terms of laying the basis for lifelong learning. There are also cases that reported aims of corporate management and economic development that might rest uneasily, if not conflict, with the more individually-oriented nurturing approach of some of the above statements:

[Mondragón] is an educational centre having close ties with the outside environment, and whose purpose is to adapt to the surrounding socio-professional reality, and to the shifting socio-economic circumstances in which we live. It offers a different conception of school organisation, since it has taken a model of corporate management and tailored it to an educational institution. [Mondragón Polytechnic School, Spain.]

Our goal is to achieve education for development, giving young peasants a high level education that prepares them to solve their problems and fulfil their needs (...). The model includes an innovative curriculum, community problem-solving activities, teacher training between peasant teachers themselves, and updating programme that modifies the proposal so that it may better respond to a changing reality in the local, regional and national contexts. [CESDER, Centre for Studies in Rural Development, Mexico.]

How far there is in fact compatibility or conflict in terms of the fundamental goals espoused by these different schools cannot be decided from these short statements. The caring environment in which the student feels secure and respected, for instance, is as compatible with social, community-based models as it is with individualistic ones where the school seeks to offer a haven of protection precisely from the perceived harmful influence of the surrounding society.

Whether the school regards itself primarily as introducing the student to the wider world, or to offer protection from it, is likely to colour the opportunities made available to develop citizenship – emphasised by Kennedy as crucial for schools in the future. Citizenship is, by its nature, socially and community-oriented. Yet, it is also these social goals that are often the most controversial in schooling; many, including some parents, stress the main purposes of schools to be in developing cognitive knowledge and skills, with social and ethical concerns only as desirable "bi-products". Hence, one major issue is how far schools should define themselves more exclusively in terms of developing cognitive abilities in the young or how far they should adopt, and be allowed to adopt, the broader social view of their purposes. The risk of following the first route may be, *pace* Kennedy, that the schools lose the interest of one of their major constituents – the students – by being viewed as irrelevant. The risk in the second route, *pace* Hargreaves, is that they may lose the support of another – the educated parent – by being regarded as offering a curriculum that is too broad and diluted.

It may further be asked how far this need be seen a choice – more stress on the cognitive entailing less on the social, ethical and emotional, and *vice versa* – or instead can both routes be developed at once? Whichever is true, the facts remain that the broader non-cognitive purposes are both more controversial and more implicit in the strategies of teachers, schools and educational policy, and yet, for many, they are *the* paramount aims. The particular focus of the Czech examples, with both cognitive and non-cognitive goals...

> *The headteachers of the schools reported equally that the goal of their school is, first of all, to raise the children to become polite and literate adults.* [NEMES, the Czech Republic.]

> *The schools aim to educate a polite citizen with her/his responsibility, knowledge of relations, tradition, landscape, and environment of the village.* [Ivancice-Reznovice Primary School, the Czech Republic.]

... includes a stress on "politeness" and "tradition" that might appall libertarians advocating greater freedom from social convention for children to develop their personal expression. It illustrates the tension that exists between schools necessarily reflecting their society, and hence to some degree reproducing it, and schools seeking to develop and liberate talents in individuals untrammelled by social patterns and inequalities. The following Mexican example also rejects the individualism of certain progressive ideals, but with a politically-informed agenda of social change:

> *Language Appropriation [is] a cross-curricular area in our education model. Its goal is to enhance ability for expression and communication by progressively mastering various languages (...). It seeks to help students and communities to overcome the "culture of silence", an old tradition that leads to remaining silent in front of authorities and city people, as well as in the face of problems, needs and injustice.* [CESDER, Centre for Studies in Rural Development, Mexico.]

Organisation and methods – new and traditional

Technological and international influences on school organisation

Two major aspects, that shape the ends, means and methods in some of the schools sampled, warrant particular focus here: schools that have integrated ICT significantly throughout their operation, and schools with a very strong international interest. Indeed, the two now often go hand in hand, for it is common now for international educational networks to be generated and maintained *via* electronic means. Two of the several sampled schools reporting a strong emphasis on the integration of ICT in their operation cover a wide age range of provision, from nursery, through primary to lower and upper secondary:

> This [is] a model of the application of new technologies in the area of nursery and primary education (...) prompting the institution to gradually modify its curriculum, its scheduling and its organisation. The school's methodological approach involves encouraging pupils to develop curiosity, critical attitudes and a tendency to seek out, through communication, in such a way that work is considered the basis for learning and, consequently, their training. ["Emili Carles-Tolrà" Nursery and Primary Schools, Barcelona, Spain.]

> The innovations at Monkseaton are based on the premise that schools must become learning organisations that will equip students to live and learn in an information society. Monkseaton does not seek to become a unique institution, but rather to help develop an integrated blend of innovative methods, partnerships and technologies that can serve as a model for any school. [Monkseaton Community High School, the United Kingdom.]

They underline that it is difficult, even meaningless, to identify the contribution of ICT separately from all the other aspects of a school's aims and methods. To look for models of the "school of tomorrow" in the comprehensive exploitation of challenging new technological possibilities might be supposed to describe a radically different form of education from previous practice. Instead, the more intensive exploitation of ICT may be more accurately viewed, in the terms of Hutmacher's analysis, as ensuring the constancy of schools as societies have moved from the industrial to the information age – adaptation rather than revolution. ICT may also in some circumstances be just as much, to use Hargreaves's terms, the medium of the "factory" model of the school as it is that of the "knowledge-creating" model that he advocates. The key question is thus not whether but how ICT is developed and used in different learning contexts by different groups of learners.

Internationalism of outlook is the other particular focus singled out in this section, as illustrated in the following two schools:

> High priority to the international perspective: the comprehensive sub-objective for the school's international projects commits the school already during the first term to offer all classes a special study tour in the second year (...). The international projects are maintained and coordinated by a special, international deputy cooperating with the international sub-committee of the school. [Norresundby Upper Secondary School, Denmark.]

> The philosophy of the school was and is to create a bilingual and bicultural institution that will combine the best of traditional Turkish education with innovative and creative western methodology and curriculum. It became the first school in Turkey to offer the International Baccalaureate (IB) Diploma. The IB Programme places strong emphasis on research, critical thinking, and the guiding premise of the "Theory of Knowledge" curriculum that requires

students to understand education and learning from an interdisciplinary point of view and to think and question actively. [Koç Özel Lisesi, Turkey.]

As with other aspects of schools life, these emphases on ICT and international-ism can be a particular curriculum strength as a valued subject alongside a number of other programmes of study, or else it can permeate the life of the school right across its operations and fields of study. Various factors may facilitate the adoption of the international profile to the school's life, including the resources available for exchange and curriculum development, teacher outlook and expertise, and com-munity attitudes. Given these different factors, international models of schools for tomorrow may well prove a much more realistic option for some schools and com-munities than others, electronic networking notwithstanding.

Moving beyond stated aims, several of the schools describe how the interna-tional and ICT priorities have shaped their operation and their teaching and learn-ing processes; the form internationalism in learning has taken includes shared programmes *via* distance learning and student electronic exchange:

To promote linguistic plurality, subjects are taught in two languages (Spanish and English) until age nine, and in three languages (French being introduced) thereafter (...). The school attaches special importance to outside excursions and activities, organising field trips in Spain, exchange programmes with its European counterparts and ongoing cultural activities: visits to exhibitions, museums, tours, discovery of the city, etc. Connection to the Internet allows stu-dents, aged ten and up, to seek out information, to work in groups with children at other schools in Spain or abroad, and to pursue specific educational objectives in the areas of math-ematics, an interest in reading, etc. [Colegio Liceo Europeo (CLE), Madrid, Spain.]

The "global classroom" offers an innovatory example by extending learning and teaching across curricular and national boundaries. Simultaneous teaching and learning is undertaken between schools in several courses based on sharing curricula. The model offers further inno-vation by encouraging extended student and staff exchange between the partner school com-munities. This brings a significant innovatory and international dimension to the project. [Anderson High School, Scotland, the United Kingdom.]

Similarly for the integration of ICT, the cases describe how this has altered organisation, curriculum, teaching, as well as the technical configurations involved:

At Hunting Hills High School, specially developed "learner guides" allow students to use computers or other learning resources to pursue independent studies. Special software helps students in career and technology studies to plan and build new products, edit video and audio productions, and much more. Access to the Internet adds a new dimension to doing research and collecting information. [Hunting Hills High School, Red Deer, Alberta, Canada.]

MEF Schools have a policy of encouraging students at all grades levels to use computers and other types of integrated communication systems efficiently and productively. For this reason, there is a computer library and nine computer laboratories including one in the kindergarten. The MEF Schools campus is a collection of eleven separate buildings designated Block A to

111

Block K. *They are interconnected via an AT&T fiber optic backbone* (...) *with MS Internet Mail Connector for internal and international e-mail thus allowing any user on campus to send and receive Internet mail. Presently, there are 250 computers on campus with plans to increase the number to 450 computers by the end of 1998.* [MEF Schools, Istanbul, Turkey.]

"The electronic school": generally the teachers involved in the project assess the results of the two years of instruction positively. It is the general experience that intensive use of computers gives far greater opportunity of differentiated teaching. [Norresundby Upper Secondary School, Denmark.]

In some cases, these kinds of interconnections extend beyond the reorganisation of the learning that takes place within the school, or between one school and another, whether in the same country or across countries, to include the links between the students and the school staff outside the normal school hours:

CLE may be the only school in Spain whose students keep in contact with the establishment, via Internet, outside of traditional school hours, since they are able to reach their teachers for guidance or help with their homework. [Colegio Liceo Europeo (CLE), Madrid, Spain.]

How far teachers in general would welcome the notion of breaking down school walls to the extent of permitting students or parents having such constant access is an open question.

Class and teaching organisation

One major reason why schools need to move away from the "factory model" of teaching and learning is that organisations in the other major sectors of society, especially the workplace, are themselves rejecting inflexible, bureaucratic structures. A key area where the old moulds most need to be broken is in the organisation of the learning interface itself. For many of the schools sampled by countries as "schools of tomorrow", cross-curricular, multi-disciplinary forms of learning have become commonplace, whether in ways that would be familiar in many schools in OECD countries, or in more radical forms...

The setting of targets and evaluation have therefore become key concepts for a reorganisation of the teaching. The formation of year group teams is of a just as central importance. Many schools find it problematic to get these teams to function, and it is our opinion that this is often due to the fact that the teachers do not consider the teams to be important. Only with the interdisciplinary/project-oriented teaching has cooperation become a necessity, and then you find very well-functioning year group teams. [Langebjergskolen Municipal Primary and Lower Secondary School, Denmark.]

As a rule, no textbooks are used; students put together their own study materials (books, monographs, CD-ROMs, video cassettes, etc.). Students may study subjects that they choose themselves. In experimental areas, the methodological process runs the gamut from practice to theoretical comprehension. The bulk of the activities by which subject matter, values and behaviour are learned involves special thematic units. The role of the teaching staff is to map out the processes of comprehension and learning (both general and personalised), expression, creativity, intellectual curiosity, the scientific method and moral and aesthetic sensitivity, in addition to monitoring and evaluating the level of knowledge acquired. The school's organisation is characterised by the maintenance of a flexible structure, with regard to the utilisation of both space and time, and by the formation of groups, which are not always stable. [Colegio Liceo Europeo (CLE), Madrid, Spain.]

Cross-curricular teaching, discovery learning, cooperative learning and project-based teaching are familiar concepts in many education systems. EBE (experience-based education) clearly includes elements of all these concepts. However, what makes EBE special is the fact it takes education organised around themes as the basis of the entire learning process, and not as one of several varieties of teaching applied in the classroom. A major condition for successful implementation is the full support of all the teachers in the school. [Apeldoorn Primary School, the Netherlands.]

... with implications for the organisation of teaching, as for example...

The school has abandoned the traditional model where whole-class teaching dominates. Instead, teaching takes place on a more individualised basis, with teachers as helpers rather than as instructors. One third of the teaching time is devoted to whole-class instruction; the remaining time pupils work independently using both textbooks and computers. The school has 60 computers for its 240 pupils. [Primary School De Notenkraker, Rotterdam, the Netherlands.]

New arrangements were introduced in 1990 as part of a large-scale reform process in primary schools: classes grouped together in twos or threes and taught by two or more teachers. The new system of teaching breaks the traditional "one teacher/one class" approach and is different from the composite system of class teacher and specialist teachers in operation in other countries. In the current school year (1997-98) the majority of pupils (85%) are taught within this new framework. Class sizes are relatively small – on average 17 pupils per class – and teacher/pupil ratios are low. [Primary Schools, Italy.]

... often combined with the re-organisation of the time available for learning:

The various classes have lessons of varying length and breaks at different points of time during the day. The school year is divided into six terms each having a teaching plan emphasizing different themes or subjects for each period of time. Some basic subjects have the same structure and volume throughout the whole school year. The periodical planning is a new practice aiming to get more variation as well as comprehensive theme and project work (...). Teamwork has become an innovative element in the Norwegian school because the curriculum implemented as a regulation demands teamwork for the individual teacher. [Arnestad Primary School, Norway.]

The pupils can decide to a large extent how to spend their learning time. The main requirements set for the pupils are that they must be present during both the contact periods and the self-study periods hours and that at the end of the week they must have finished their week task. To monitor pupils' progress, the school has designed an elaborate pupil monitor-

113

ing system, which makes it possible to check progress with great precision. Each pupil forms part of a mentor group of maximally six pupils. Within this group there are intensive contacts between the mentor and individual pupils. [Carolus Borromeus College, Helmond, the Netherlands.]

To provide maximum flexibility for individual students, the school's timetable includes full year, semestered and quarter-mestered courses as well as independent study or self-directed courses. There are no bells in the school because programmes are not based on rigidly established blocks of time. [Hunting Hills High School, Red Deer, Alberta, Canada.]

Full attention is paid to cultivating independence and autonomy of the pupils rather than controlling and supervising them. For instance, while it is a very common practice in Japan's school for bells to chime the opening and ending of classes, no bell rings in this school at all with a view toward fostering children who can manage time by themselves in daily life where no signal tells them when and what to do. [Utase Elementary School, Japan.]

The schools refuse time pressure and try to use the time more effectively instead – in longer blocks, for longer concentration of children, possibility of individual approach and co-operative learning. [NEMES, the Czech Republic.]

After school hours, they offer a range of cultural, sports and educational activities for pupils, parents and other people living in the neighbourhood (…). Broad schools are often open until late at night and they often stay open during the weekend and during school holidays. [Primary School De Notenkraker, Rotterdam, the Netherlands.]

These extracts offer insights into some of the ways in which the schools in question have re-organised their learning resources. They are illustrative of the many imaginative ways in which schools more broadly are responding to new challenges. There is variation across education systems in the extent to which schools enjoy such room for manœuvre, and the tolerance or promotion of diversity among schools. The Introduction has already referred to the strong pressures that can inhibit experimentation in favour of the familiar. An important factor here is the strong influence exerted in some countries by evaluation, assessment and examination regimes away from a willingness to innovate and experiment. There is a question too of how far the schools and teachers possess the necessary skills and attitudes for these broader definitions of professionalism. The support they receive from parents and the community in favour of particular innovative strategies is vital.

The traditional alongside the new

In a number of the reported school cases, more traditional aims and methods are explicitly mentioned as co-existing with radical experiment and novel re-organisation. This is even expressed as a lesson learned from experiment: that it can be tempting to lose sight of the importance of established values in the rush to change, so that a new balance needs to be found between them. These lessons have been learned by schools from as far apart as Denmark and Canada:

> The latest technological equipment and pedagogical theories are combined with firm discipline policies, clearly expressed objectives and high standards of achievement. Although education needs to change to stay relevant, learning is still learning (...). Technology is used only when it is the most appropriate and effective tool for learning, teaching and operating the school. If a pencil and paper, or the telephone, will do the job more quickly and easily, then the computers are put aside so that people who really need them can have adequate access. [Hunting Hills High School, Red Deer, Alberta, Canada.]

> Monkseaton is creating a new learning environment that combines the best of traditional teaching and learning with: lifelong learning skills and attitudes; appropriate technology, especially communications and information technologies; access to the new learning environment in school and at home; partnerships with industry, the community, and students themselves. The benefits of rigorous evaluation are central to the philosophy of learning at Monkseaton: learning what does not work is as important as learning what will. The evaluations are based on external measures, such as national examinations. Another important evaluation is that of attitudes, where there has been a significant shift in favour of working with IT, and working abroad. [Monkseaton Community High School, the United Kindgom.]

> The project has been running now for some two years, and some experience has already emerged demonstrating many advantages in IT-assisted instruction, and equally important, experience demonstrating the necessity of circumspection where methodology is concerned, and when the use of computers is less appropriate or downright distracting to the teaching process. [Norresundby Upper Secondary School, Denmark.]

Despite shared perceptions in these cases, some of the examples of "schools of tomorrow" also express conflicting values. The introduction of the school uniform was reported in a Scottish school (St. Luke's High School, Glasgow) as an integral part of the change that had turned it into a more dynamic and effective institution, while in a Turkish school it is regarded as the opposite [We believe that wearing a certain uniform limits a person's personal development (MEF Schools, Istanbul, Turkey)]. There are many possible paths for schools for tomorrow, not a single model. As Cros advises in her chapter, different practices should be understood in terms of the context that generated them. What might be new and liberating in one system might be well-tried, even tired, in another.

The key role of teachers

The point is repeatedly underlined in these cases how vital is the teaching staff to the success of innovative practices. They are perceived as critical to maintaining the momentum so that changed practice becomes part of the normal functioning of the school. Not surprisingly, the importance identified for the teacher's role goes hand-in-hand with a strong emphasis on professional development, especially in-service for those already in post. For example:

> To promote the motivation and professionalisation of the teachers, the school has adopted a personnel policy based on the theory of human resources management. This means, among other things, that teachers are given ample opportunity to work on their professional development. [Apeldoorn Primary School, the Netherlands.]

> High priority to in-service training of the teachers and the management. Pedagogic days are held (on Saturdays), and every second year a pedagogic week-end, both involving external lecturers and teachers. Pedagogic study groups are held and internal teaching supervision by colleagues has been established. A special library for educational literature has been established and new publications are advertised in the weekly journals. [Norresundby Upper Secondary School, Denmark.]

As in a recent CERI study (CERI/OECD, 1998b), the schools tend to operate with the broad notion of in-service professional development (not just formal INSET), to emphasise that the professional learning in question is often informal and collective not just what takes place when an individual teacher attends a training course.

To focus on teachers is, of course, nothing new. Despite longstanding acknowledgement of their importance, teachers are still not always equipped or motivated to meet such new demands, nor does the culture of schooling in all places encourage the dialogues to flourish that permit schools to become "learning organisations". Moreover, some regard teachers as much as "part of the problem as of the solution", suggesting that there is yet no unanimity about the nature of their professionalism and the level of trust they enjoy. For many of the schools being featured in this Appendix, however, that primacy of the teacher's role is clear:

> It is important to emphasise that the school's entire teaching staff is involved in the project in one way or another, through either the computer class or the classroom computer. In addition, all of them have taken various training courses, and, at the same time, three of the teachers are themselves trainers in this area (...). It can be considered that this experiment could be generalised easily, inasmuch as it does not call for especially extraordinary material resources. It depends solely on the motivation and coordinated effort of the teaching staff. ["Emili Carles-Tolrà" Nursery and Primary Schools, Barcelona, Spain.]

> Knowing students, determining their lacking points, assessing the system, feeding back, identifying the attitudes of children and orientation for future by evaluation and assessment, not accepting evaluation and assessment as the helmet of passing examinations and success in exams. Creating learning school – learning organisation dynamics by attaching importance to in-service training of teachers and executives. [Irmak, Turkey.]

> Change was prompted by the high dropout rate, but the debate about how to reduce dropout soon extended to include the general quality of teaching (...). Educational changes included a stronger focus on pupil guidance and the role of teachers in that respect. Teachers have become supervisors who guide the learning process and who, much more so than in the past,

116

keep track of individual learning outcomes. Teachers are now expected to solve or at least to discuss the problems pupils may have, instead of just giving low marks and ignoring the underlying problems. [Carolus Borromeus College, Helmond, the Netherlands.]

Knowledge is being created rather than transmitted in the school. The teacher often functions rather as a coordinator. Work in the projects fosters and manifests better communication skills; ability to evaluate, take, and defend a position; co-operative behaviour. [Brumovice Primary School, the Czech Republic.]

The range of tasks and areas of development that are implied for the teacher is indeed wide. They should be at once knowledgeable about subject matter; able to organise learning and motivate students using the gamut of learning possibilities now available; provide guidance and act as channels of interaction with parents and the community; informed about new methodologies for teaching and learning and able to apply them to their own contexts; act in very close collaboration with colleagues in the solution of organisational, pedagogical and pastoral issues. Some teachers have always adhered to such demanding definitions of professionalism; these examples suggest that this is coming increasingly to be regarded as the norm for all. The reference in the Czech example to the school as "knowledge-creating" rather than "knowledge-transmitting" echoes the emphasis laid by Hargreaves in Chapter 3, a direction for development that many schools are ill-equipped to pursue. Again, schools can scarcely move significantly in this direction unless teachers share this vision for teaching and learning, possess the skills and aptitudes to transform the vision into reality, and unless the system in which they operate endorses this as a key objective.

One dimension that may well be changing over time is the extent to which notions of professionalism and professional responsibility are viewed primarily as matters for the individual teacher or instead as a collective enterprise. The cases reviewed in this Appendix contain many examples where successful innovation and change have depended on sustained collective endeavours by all the school's community of professionals and other key players. The Italian case, on the introduction of team-teaching across Italian primary schools, shows how even change towards more collective approaches that enjoys the support of legislation is not straightforward when this runs up against ingrained habits. Changing actual practice, as Cros observes at the beginning of Chapter 4, is much more challenging than altering either structures or rhetoric.

Debates are in progress over the reform. Issues concern implementation and the added value of the system of teaching in teams as compared with traditional arrangements. Quality of interaction among teachers: the transition from an individual approach to a team approach takes time, is difficult, implies in-depth cultural change and requires large scale in-service training programmes (…). [Primary Schools, Italy.]

It might be supposed that moving in the direction of "student-centred" learning, with the teacher as facilitator, reduces the professional demands on teachers

117|

by focusing on other aspects of the teacher/learner interaction. The opposite seems to be much nearer the mark: the introduction of demanding, flexible schedules and individualised methods for learning, increases not reduces the complexity and expertise demanded of teachers. Open methods, creating new knowledge not just transmitting the tried and tested, rely on still more preparation and understanding of teaching strategies, not less:

> A major lesson learned in this context is that the introduction of the study house should be extremely well prepared. The teaching methods used in the model require further consideration. There is a strong need for the further development of methods that are appropriate for this new educational concept. This goes particularly for the use of information and communication technologies, including the Internet. [Carolus Borromeus College, Helmond, the Netherlands.]

> If the pupil is to be more active and assume joint responsibility for his or her work, the teacher must have the courage to let go of the very detailed control and leave some of the initiatives to the pupil. It does not mean that the teacher is to let the pupil take over the responsibility for the teaching. But if the pupils are working more independently, it requires that the teacher has a much greater overview and awareness of the content of the teaching. [Langebjergskolen Municipal Primary and Lower Secondary School, Denmark.]

The point needs to be emphasised in relation to the use of ICT. Far from reducing the role of the teacher as the learning facilitator and strategist, the successful deployment of ITC makes still more demands on his or her skills as an individual, and on the collective organisation of learning in the school as a whole. It is not, as some might hope, a "cheap alternative".

Finally, some cases refer to the use made of staff who have come *via* non-traditional routes, opening up the issue of "who" the teacher is and should be in the schools of tomorrow (see also next section on community interaction):

> The school makes use of the opportunity created by the government to appoint long-term unemployed people in subsidised posts; 18 people now hold such a post, for instance as assistants or as maintenance staff. The school also uses volunteers, including teachers who contribute to the after-school activities. [Primary School De Notenkraker, Rotterdam, the Netherlands.]

> All the areas must be applied to community life. With the agreement of parents and students, knowledge coming from research workshops and technological training must be applied at home in order to pass the courses. Thus, the effects of education on community are almost guaranteed because parents work in applying knowledge and, many times, teach at school or learn from their children. [CESDER, Centre for Studies in Rural Development, Mexico.]

How far should change in school practice go hand in hand with change in definitions of who the teacher is, whether from the viewpoint of recruitment profiles or from that of professional and legal status? Can new sources of expertise be drawn on from outside the ranks of the teaching force that will enhance not diminish the quality of learning? The issues raised here are complex and controversial. The involvement of outsiders may well be invaluable in opening up the horizons to the wider world and to help loosen otherwise rigid moulds of educational practice. But how far does it also run the risk that the perception of teaching as requiring high quality, high-level capabilities might be undermined, consistent with the "bright person" myth that wrongly supposes that anyone of intelligence can step into a teaching/learning environment? So the general question is: can the opening up of what is understood as "school knowledge" be speeded up by drawing on the expertise of others in ways that do not diminish either the recognition and motivations of teachers or the quality of teaching and learning? These are likely to be increasingly addressed issues in the future.

The schools' links to their different communities

Schools, parents, local communities

Opening up classrooms to parents and other adults is one expression of close school-community linkages. A strong emphasis found in many of the country cases is their activity as community centres:

> The system of after school activities is an integrated part of Reform 97, which is a family reform as well. All municipalities are to provide for activities, care and supervision for children between 6-9 before and after school. At Arnestad approximatively 170 pupils daily use this system (...). The cultural aspect of Reform 97 emphasises activities in the local community to become part of the daily school life. [Arnestad Primary School, Norway.]

> Another unique concept of this school is "school as a centre for community development". Utase elementary school is expected to play an important role as a community centre as well as actively to encourage strong community (...). An open system is employed with no fences built around the school, no walls installed between classrooms and corridors, or even no movable partitions used. On holidays local residents are allowed to use the gymnasium and play ground (...). A school bulletin is distributed by the pupils not only to their parents/guardians but also local residents who have no child enrolled in the school. Community people are also encouraged to participate in school events such as an athletic meeting. Extra-curricular activities are organised by the school once or twice a term where local people who have special knowledge and skills are invited as instructors to teach pupils. This is one of the examples of community support for the school, but more unique feature to this activity is that parents/guardians are also encouraged to take part in the class together with their children. [Utase Elementary School, Japan.]

> De Notenkraker ("The Nutcracker") is an example of a "broad" school [and] is also a "digital" school, with various innovative applications of modern technology. The essence of the "broad school" concept is that these schools, besides being regular teaching institutions, function as a centre of activities for the neighbourhood. After school hours, they offer a range of cultural,

sports and educational activities for pupils, parents and other people living in the neighbourhood. This leads to fruitful cooperation between the school and other agencies. It also results in unusual opening hours: broad schools are often open until late at night and they often stay open during the weekend and during school holidays.

In the past school year every day some 75 people from the neighbourhood participated in a wide range of cultural, social, sports and educational activities. About 40% of the people attending these activities have no direct relation with the school. The contacts between the school and the community are increasing. From each ethnic group, there is at least one parent who is actively involved in the after-school activities and who often serves as a contact person with the ethnic community of which he/she is a member. [Primary School De Notenkraker, Rotterdam, the Netherlands.]

Parents in the village community showed a lot of interests and have called for establishment of schools and are prepared to build the school themselves with bush materials. The elementary school children respected their teachers because they belong to the same village community and speak the same tokpeles. [Papua New Guinea.]

As with the vital role of good teachers, there is nothing essentially new about community involvement in the life of schools nor about recognition that a valuable ingredient of educational effectiveness is the active co-operation of parents and the wider community. This could just as well be said of schools of yesterday as of today and tomorrow. School-community relations are nevertheless undergoing important, if variable, change. What the "community" refers to has altered, in some cases – as encapsulated in the Scottish example of the "global classroom" – this can now extend internationally. Traditional communities, based on close ties of kinship and low geographical mobility, remain in place in some parts of the OECD countries while they are breaking down rapidly in others. The position of the school and of the teacher are being transformed by all these changes. Its community role might have been strengthened, as expressed by Kennedy in Chapter 1, by the fragmentation of many aspects of modern life, while to the extent that parents in general are now much more educated than in times gone by this is one factor serving to diminish the special status of the school as the repository of local wisdom.

Employers and corporations

One section of the community has proved to be especially valuable for schools – major employers, particularly those involved in the manufacture or distribution of ICT products – *inter alia*, for extending facilities and improving links with the world of employment:

This means that competing hardware suppliers or content providers work side by side to develop, in Monkseaton, a test site that will allow them to evaluate future developments. At the same time, the publicity opportunities that arise offer an immediate chance to advance corporate interests. The interaction of hardware suppliers and content producers with the users at Monkseaton creates a creative development centre that allows all those involved to trial new ideas and processes. [Monkseaton Community High School, the United Kingdom.]

Another key resource in this school is the community. Hunting Hills has developed partnerships and associations locally with Red Deer College, a merchants association, the chamber of commerce, a theatre company, sporting groups and businesses. The school also has mutually beneficial relationships with major corporations such as Pepsi, Canon-Lion (Ikon) Business Machines, Honda and Apple Canada. [Hunting Hills High School, Red Deer, Alberta, Canada.]

"The electronic school" in 1994 we were asked as one of two schools to participate in the project of the Ministry of Education, "The electronic school". The project is to a great extent financed by the Ministry of Education and the main sponsors Apple Macintosh and Telecom Denmark, but the school also contributes considerably out of its own funds. [Norresundby Upper Secondary School, Denmark.]

Promoting such links depends on a measure of entrepeneurialism on the part of the school, and may be encouraged, as in the Danish case, by government support. While the involvement of commercial interests in school life can raise ethical issues about interests and control, for the above schools at least the relationships appear to be fruitful. They represent an important extension of the school's community while providing an invaluable input of resources and expertise. The potential of such links to contribute in related fields – such as improving aspects of curriculum relevance and broadening teacher professional development opportunities – can also be imagined.

Post-school education institutions

Certain of these schools report strong connections with another part of their community that is still closer to the educational enterprise – post-school education and training institutions. Again, this is not unusual or specific to these particular schools. What is perhaps unusual in some of the schools selected is the degree to which many successful or innovative features are combined together, and the strength of the ties that they enjoy with these partners of their communities (such as ICT suppliers or higher education institutions):

At Monkseaton students routinely start university two years early. This arises from an innovative partnership with the Open University. The Open University offered the school the best starting model for a successful lifelong learning institution. The students benefit from a staged introduction to university studies, learning new study skills, an early demonstration of their ability at this level (all students have gone on to their first choice university), and greater confidence in different learning environments. [Monkseaton Community High School, the United Kingdom.]

Students who are working at advanced levels can also take college courses at the school, in a regular class along with adult students who are enrolled in college (...). Students may opt to take independent study courses offered by the Alberta Distance Learning Centre. [Hunting Hills High School, Red Deer, Alberta, Canada.]

What is being described in these two cases is in effect an extension of the level and programme range that the school can offer through the close links developed with tertiary programmes. Still closer links have been developed in the following cases in Mexico and Spain, as part of rural development centres that have extended the school-based element into advanced post-school teaching and research:

CES *operates from grade seven (lower secondary schools) to college (...). The model's success is based upon the work of these young professionals, who studied with* CES *and today teach at the school or promote environmental, agricultural, micro-enterprises or organisation projects. All of them are high-level professionals: during their studies they work with other students, researchers and teachers from universities and research institutions from Mexico and other countries.* [CESDER, Centre for Studies in Rural Development, Mexico.]

Created by private initiative in 1943 as a vocational school, the institution expanded and developed into a training centre and, thanks to the enthusiasm of its young people, became a cooperative enterprise. In 1966, MEP set up an innovative unit called Actividad Laboral Escolar Cooperativa (Cooperative Work Study Programme, or Alecop), which enables students to combine study with work experience. In 1968, MEP gained official recognition for its technical engineering course (involving three years of post-secondary study). In 1977, the Ikerlan research centre was established; today, with over 200 researchers, it is one of the Spain's leading technological centres. Lastly, in 1985, DIARIA (an industrial design institute) was set up thanks to cooperation between a variety of institutions. Today MEP can be considered an administrative hybrid: while basically a private cooperative, responsibility for the school is shared with Caja Laboral Popular (a credit union) and the General Council of Guipúzcoa province. [Mondragón Polytechnic School, Spain.]

The location of the schools in broader programmes and research centres clearly impacts on the curriculum and teaching resources available through the specialist focus of the centres, while ensuring very strong ties with the community and local economy. The very meaning of what constitutes a "school" is raised, with new configurations available for the management of knowledge and the interpretation of lifelong learning.

Networking and innovation

The school or schools of the future?

One of the previous examples, the CESDER in Mexico, illustrates how a number of the school cases do not correspond to the simple model of the single institution bounded by its own location, personnel and students. Many of them are integrated into networks that have been developed either in contribution to a broader initiative or as emerging from the grass-roots as a more effective way of combining learning resources:

The programme is based on "creating educational situations", a model in practice in a small indigenous region south-central Mexico since 1982. The creating educational situations

(CES) *model operates in a region in which two of the poorest municipalities in Mexico are located. It works in eleven secondary schools (grades 7 to 9) and three preparatory schools (grades 10 to 12). There is also a College Programme in Rural Development planning. The schools are located in communities between 800 and 1 500 inhabitants.* [CESDER, Centre for Studies in Rural Development, Mexico.]

The "global classroom" is currently a partnership of six schools reflecting six varied communities [in Shetland Islands, Scotland, Sweden, Germany, the Czech Republic, South Africa, Japan]. The model is based on senior students in each school using information technology to share visions, ideas, information and materials on themes significant to the coming millennium. These are agreed to by students, teachers and partnership communities. [Anderson High School, Scotland, the United Kingdom.]

In a pilot phase they began to study the energy situation in their school building and in their own homes. A year later they tackled a major task: to analyze the use of energy in four small villages (the home communities of most of the pupils) (...). The next step appeared to be a logical consequence; to link up with other schools and to find solutions for a number of new questions (...). From 1991 to 1994 almost thirty schools had taken over the idea to contribute to the development of an energy policy in their communities. [Bundesrealgymnasium of Imst, Austria.]

Despite the obvious benefits that networking can bring, it can also be an energy-consuming process with often uncertain results. Outcomes can depend critically on the motivation of an individual or groups of individuals, or the impetus of an inspirational objective, as in the Austrian example above. The networking might refer to particular thematic projects or entail broader across-the-board co-operation with others.

While innovation often springs from local grass-roots initiative it can also be stimulated or supported by broader programmes, which support might be essential to its continuation:

An area of focal interest in developing learning and communication among disabled pupils is making the use of information technology and data communications readily available to them. To this end a project has been launched and includes eight state-owned special schools along with an action network comprising several municipality-owned regional schools (...). The projects are being carried out mainly by individual schools and associations of schools throughout Finland. In addition to providing monetary support, the role of the Finnish National Board of Education is [co-ordination and] to ensure the effectiveness and transmitting of experiences to the field of education as a whole via follow-up groups established in most projects. [DATERO programme, Finland.]

For almost two years, students have been learning modern languages through video conferencing with students in other countries. The school has put video conferencing machines in partner schools in Lille, Hamburg, and La Coruna, and students on all sites have regular timetabled slots where they converse with peers on a range of subjects (...). In the case of Introduction to the Information Society course, fifty schools in the United Kingdom and

Europe have been given access to an intranet with the course and some supporting materials available on it. [Monkseaton Community High School, the United Kingdom.]

How dependent are the networks on such broader impetus and support? Would they otherwise wither away for lack of the organisational capacity provided from the centre, or the necessary financial resources, or simply the symbolic importance of belonging to the wider project? Even where there is dependency, it is not necessarily indicative of collaboration that is weakly-rooted or short-lived, and indeed it suggests a valuable role of policy initiatives in providing support to sustain grass-roots collaboration.

Networks, here called "school bushes", are also reported as an important feature of recent Hungarian developments:

Little schools are peculiar to Hungarian educational system. However, the comprehensive functioning can be satisfactory only in large schools. This is the contradiction which we try to eliminate by organisation of school associations. Leader experts of the innovation develop propositions and improvements projects for the schools and "school bushes" on the fields of the curriculum, the inner functioning, the instructional design, the in-service training of teachers and the educational assessment. For example in this innovation some relatively new outcomes of researches play a significant role. We try to introduce new and revolutionary visions of learning, especially the constructivism, we implement techniques of curriculum development counted as brand new ones in Hungary, we change the rigid, one-sided, discipline oriented nature of instruction and curriculum. [Hungary.]

The network is regarded, despite or perhaps because of the inertia within the system, as an important means of developing the "economies of scale" and a broader range of options possible with larger educational units without abandoning the Hungarian tradition of the small school. The "school bush" is regarded as a potentially highly effective channel of educational change.

Processes of innovation

Innovation is engendered and sustained through very different routes. Despite the over-simplification of the "top-down vs. bottom up" contrast (see Cros, Chapter 4), the cases show how it might at least be "top-inspired"...

This secondary school started some years ago to look for ways to promote independent learning in the upper forms. The model that is now being used to this end is called the "study house", a novel concept of learning introduced by national policy. [Carolus Borromeus College, Helmond, the Netherlands.]

The Multimedia Super Corridor (MSC) will be a multimedia "island of excellence" comprising a system of capabilities, technologies, legislation, infrastructure and policies designed to give the users a unique competitive advantage in the development, integration and use of multimedia technologies. The MSC has set "Eight Flagship Applications" destined to become the R&D centres for the information-based industries in the borderless world of the next millennium. One of the Flagship Applications is "The smart school" where the use of leading edge technology will be emphasised in the teaching and learning processes. The concept of "smart school" will be pioneered by ninety selected schools all over the nation in January 1999. [Malaysia.]

... as well as begin and develop through the initiative of small number of individual teachers:

The systematic work in tutorial teams started in 1994 when 9 teachers from 2 different classes decided to work together (...). In 1995 six new tutorial teams were started in addition to the team that continued from the year before. It was, however, no longer an experiment funded from other sources. The new teams consisted of teachers who had wanted to work together in this way themselves. In 1996, there were tutorial teams with all first-year classes at Viborg Amtsgymnasium, and this year (1997-98) tutorial teams have been established in all first and second year classes (altogether 21 classes). [Viborg Upper Secondary School, Denmark.]

In a secondary school in the Tyrol, Austria, a biology teacher (Mag Gottfried Mair) started an "energy network" with a group of 14-year-old students (...). The teacher who had initiated the energy network originally gained a high reputation, won with his students a number of national and international awards, and was offered financial and infrastructural support through the authorities. [Bundesrealgymnasium of Imst, Austria.]

Beyond the intent of the first (about 40) teachers' gathering to exchange ideas how to reach such aim, it evolved into a broad innovative stream of schools and individual teachers, with a shared philosophy and methods consistent with that philosophy. [NEMES, the Czech Republic.]

These examples alone give an insight into how relatively small-scale beginnings can gather momentum, acquiring their own institutional basis and significance within the system as a whole. As if to illustrate the over-simplification of the "top-down" and "bottom-up" contrast, the Viborg extract describes a teacher-led initiative that then drew on national funding for its development, before further developing through a broader range of players within the school environment.

The role of the principal, as a key intermediary and actor in ensuring the launch of innovation, is mentioned in a number of the cases, *e.g.*:

Teachers who were used to having their classroom to themselves when the lessons were finished, were now asked to give up their room for after-school activities. This evoked some resistance. Because the changes were introduced under inspiring leadership, most teachers were motivated to contribute to the new school concept. [Primary School De Notenkraker, Rotterdam, the Netherlands.]

The head teacher suggested to staff in St Luke's that such a technique [Mind-Mapping] could have substantial advantages for our students in terms of both creating ideas and retrieving information across many areas of the curriculum (...). St Luke's High School has, through building a steady contact over the past two and a half years with Mindstore, been

125

able to bring about an almost unique situation where The Learning Game, now the focus of such international interest, is being piloted in the school by twenty-one of St Luke's staff trained through Mindstore. [St. Luke's High School, Glasgow, the United Kingdom.]

The intermediaries may well be more than a single individual (such as a school principal), as illustrated by the Scottish case. The very nature of the innovation itself might be transformed as it is developed. In the Austrian case, what started out as an educational project, launched by a single dynamic teacher, turned increasingly into a network of community initiatives albeit with an educational component:

Gradually the network newspaper (originally school-based) became a newspaper of community environmental projects. The teacher's main interest became the creation of local groups with broad participation and strong emphasis on the training of local coordinators (…). Although schools are still playing an important role, the main thrust is in establishing local groups which provide continuity and in linking the local coordinators into a regional network in order to facilitate training and the exchange of experience. [Bundesrealgymnasium of Imst, Austria.]

Not only is the network now much larger than the original initiative in terms of numbers of players and mechanisms, but so has its target and purpose been significantly widened.

Some of the most revealing statements in the country cases refer to difficulties encountered, that were problematic for these particular schools and which might well have been sufficient in many cases to disrupt further progress:

In our opinion there is nothing of what has been described in this report that could not in principle be done by other schools (…). The greatest challenge, however, is the establishment of sustainable consensus among all parties involved. This is the difficult part – also at Norresundby Gymnasium og HF-kursus. [Norresundby Upper Secondary School, Denmark.]

There are, of course, difficulties. Schools are not generally rewarded for changing, and there are few incentives for radical transformation. [Monkseaton Community High School, the United Kingdom.]

With regard to the process of innovation, decisions taken in expanding very good teaching practices proved to be crucial [but] two stumbling blocks may be identified. First, radical and relevant changes need support, assistance and in-service training, whereas resources are not always easily available, particularly if the process is being implemented on a large scale. Second, policy by mandate generates mediocrity and opposition; very demanding tasks require excellence in initial training, in-depth expertise and an attitude of professionalism, conditions that are not necessarily easy to find. [Primary Schools, Italy.]

A major potential difficulty in implementing the concept is the change in the teaching culture that needs to take place. The Carolus College did this by implementing the concept for all subjects and all pupils (in the classes concerned) at the same time, instead of opting for a tentative try-out phase. This also precluded the possibility of attempts by unwilling teachers to hinder the process from the position of outsider. [Carolus Borromeus College, Helmond, the Netherlands.]

There are many shared ideas across the different settings about what can go wrong or represent a hurdle in the spread of innovative practice: the inertia of teachers and others unconvinced of the need for change; lack of resources; shortage of the demanding attributes needed to make change effective; the culture of systems that do not offer incentives for change, and may even provide disincentives. In the Dutch example, the way of tackling such manifold hurdles was decided to be through bold change. The Danish example usefully refers to the need to establish "sustainable consensus" – if that consensus is either unsustainable or lacking altogether the chances of generating innovative change are substantially reduced.

Innovative schools in favoured or disadvantaged environments?

While some of the country cases hint at problems and lack of initial agreement among staff and others, the general picture they convey tends to be very positive. In part, this reflects, as Cros observes, the advocate's desire to focus on the positive; in part, it reflects a genuine picture of excellence and innovation. But this then raises a further question: how far are the selected schools representative, and, if they are not, how generalisable are their experiences? For, it is clear that these examples are not fully representative of all schools.

There are a number of examples among the country cases of schools that are small:

Compared with the other high schools, the size is exceptionally small. While the average number of students of the high schools in Korea is about 1 209 as of 1996, there are only 52 students in the YSS. [Yungsan Sung-Jee School for Students At-risk, Korea.]

This is a small public school with 200 pupils ranging in age from three to eleven. There are nine teachers. ["Emili Carles-Tolrà" Nursery and Primary Schools, Barcelona, Spain.]

The number of children is 36 persons. The number of classes is 4 classes. The number of school personnel is 9 persons. [Yukinishi Elementary School, Japan.]

Village school of a small size, attended by 46 students (Ivanèice-Øeznovice), 80 students (Brumovice) and 145 students (Obøistvi). The two smaller schools are only elementary (up to the 5th grade). [NEMES, the Czech Republic.]

Not all the featured schools, however, fall into this category:

With its 794 students, 88 teachers and 11 technical and administrative staff members Norresundby Gymnasium og HF-kursus is a very large school indeed. [Norresundby Upper Secondary School, Denmark.]

127|

CLE *is a private school which was founded 25 years ago. Its 1 200 students range from 3-year-olds to those old enough to enter university.* [Colegio Liceo Europeo, Madrid, Spain.]

Some of the schools clearly enjoy particularly attractive facilities or location:

Arnestad school is a fairly new primary school (established in 1992) situated in a suburb municipality 13 miles from Oslo. The school has a suitable outdoor environment, with large playground, trees and varied landscape. [Arnestad Primary School, Norway.]

It could be said that this is a relatively wealthy area. It should be mentioned as well that this school is intended to be an experimental attempt at a possible new type of school in the future and a model for other schools, and thus it seems that the school is relatively favourably treated in financial and human resources allocation. [Utase Elementary School, Japan.]

Before beginning construction of Hunting Hills High School in 1994, the school board selected the future principal and invited him to provide input during the earliest planning stages. As a result, this facility is specifically designed to support the types of education programmes being offered at the school. The school's state-of-the-art facilities, which include 400 computers for a student body of 1 200, do not lock the staff into offering only one kind of programme. Staff, who each have an office area equipped with a computer and telephone, use computer software to track students' progress and attendance, to make announcements in the school, to communicate with each other, prepare lessons and for many other purposes. [Hunting Hills High School, Red Deer, Alberta, Canada.]

And, several are located in areas where the parents are largely comfortable with educated backgrounds:

Most of the school's pupils come from middle and upper class families. [Carolus Borromeus College, Helmond, the Netherlands.]

The population segment belongs to the wealthier part of the Danish population and is primarily career oriented. This population segment is very demanding and asks for good quality from the public service. Many parents in this segment choose a private school for their children; but in the district to which Langebjergskolen belongs, the private school enrolment is remarkably low, i.e. approximatively 9 per cent. [Langebjergskolen Municipal Primary and Lower Secondary School, Denmark.]

Hunting Hills High Schools serves a largely middle class student population in grades 9 through 12 (14 to 18 years old). [Hunting Hills High School, Red Deer, Alberta, Canada.]

Apeldoorn does not have large concentrations of groups at risk. The part of the city where De Bundel is situated also has few social problems. [Apeldoorn Primary School, the Netherlands.]

The school is located in a Madrid neighbourhood in which the socio-economic level is high. The major difficulties for implementing an experiment of this type stem from the size of the economic investment involved, on the part of the school and the families alike. [Colegio Liceo Europeo (CLE), Madrid, Spain.]

Even reports within the case studies themselves sometimes suggest that their own successes may be extremely difficult to replicate in less advantaged circumstances.

Even so, not all the sampled schools fall into these relatively favoured categories. Some are large schools, in areas of greater concentration of "at-risk" factors, and may indeed be contributing to broader policy initiatives to tackle social exclusion:

The average income of the people living in the neighbourhood is low; many people live on social security. Some 40% are immigrants. The National Metropolitan Policy programme launched by the Dutch government makes extra money available for improving the living conditions in deprived city districts. As part of the policy, support was provided for experiments with the broad school model. [Primary School De Notenkraker, Rotterdam, the Netherlands.]

St. Luke's High School is a six-year, Roman Catholic, comprehensive co-educational high school. 560 pupils are drawn from the school's catchment area with a number travelling, by parental choice, from other urban and rural locations. The catchment areas are of mixed socio-economic status, including areas of deprivation. [St. Luke's High School, Glasgow, the United Kingdom.]

The creating educational situations (CES) model operates in a region in which two of the poorest municipalities in Mexico are located. It works in eleven secondary schools (grades 7 to 9) and three preparatory schools (grades 10 to 12). There is also a College Programme in Rural Development planning. [CESDER, Centre for Studies in Rural Development, Mexico.]

In the hypotheses put forward by Hargreaves in Chapter 3, there is a pressure to innovate in situations of social polarisation and in the face of diversity and challenge. This would suggest that the dynamic, innovative school is as much to be found in social adversity as amid affluence. On the strength of these examples, however, that may be an excessively optimistic reading. They tend instead to enjoy a variety of advantages. Insofar as this can be generalised, the equity issues are obvious: not only do some schools experience greater hurdles in terms of the background of pupils and the support of their immediate communities but they may also be less likely the flexible, innovative "learning organisations" that resemble the model "schools of tomorrow". Is there a risk, in moving towards more innovative, flexible institutions, of widening still further the disparities between schools? If so, this would have profound consequences for the overall system of education and for society in general.

OECD 1999

Notes

1. The study was part of the Pacific Circle Consortium's Schooling for the Twenty First Century Project.
2. "In this way, pragmatic, progressive and liberal ideologies (...) compete to determine what we mean by education and what the role of education in society should be, while particular educational ideologies in dominance (and in becoming dominant) find alliance with particular dominant economic and political ideals and practices, sometimes sharing similar sets of assumptions and sometimes not." (Gale, 1994, p. 9)
3. Much of this chapter is based on two sources of information: the European Observatory of Innovations in Education and Training which operates under the direction of the *Institut national de recherche pédagogique*, Paris, France (the author is the Research Director); the cases prepared for the CERI/Japan Hiroshima seminar.
4. The collected data depend heavily on those who conducted the survey (university social science academics in the country in question) and on the key persons who were interviewed. The latter were senior officials of the European Union countries. In addition, the study drew on mostly official documentation, relating, for example, to legislation, or to associations and trade unions.
5. The German national correspondent observed: "The days of great reforms and innovation were the 1970s, the time of the coalition between the Social Democratic Party and the Liberals under Chancellor Willy Brandt. Today, though, political partners like political parties and pressure groups and senior officials in the *Länder* and the Federation are aware that none of the great costly reforms has achieved the legitimation and objectives that existed at the outset (...)." Accordingly, "(...) the word has gone down in people's estimation due to the poor results that actions have achieved, and particularly in view of the amount of emotional, financial and symbolic investment that went into it".

References

ALTER, N. (1996),
  Sociologie de l'entreprise et de l'innovation, PUF, Paris.

BONAMI, M. and GARANT, M. (1996),
  Systèmes scolaires et pilotage de l'innovation : émergence et implantation du changement, De Boeck University, Leuven, Belgium.

BORTHWICK, A. (1993),
  "Key competences – Uncovering the bridge between general and vocational", in C. Collins (ed.), *Competencies*, Australian College of Education, Canberra.

CERI/OECD (1997),
  Education at a Glance – OECD Indicators, 1997 Edition, Paris.

CERI/OECD (1998a),
  "Teachers for tomorrow's schools", *Educational Policy Analysis*, 1998 Edition, Paris.

CERI/OECD (1998b),
  Staying Ahead: In-service Training and Teacher Professional Development, Paris.

CROS, F. (1996),
  "Définitions et fonctions de l'innovation pédagogique ; le cas de la France de 1960 à 1994", in M. Bonami and M. Garant (eds.), *Systèmes scolaires et pilotage de l'innovation : émergence et implantation du changement*, De Boeck University, Leuven, Belgium.

CROS, F. (1998),
  "L'innovation en éducation et formation : vers la construction d'un objet de recherche ?", *Éducation permanente*, No. 133, Paris.

DAWKINS, J.S. (1988),
  Strengthening Australia's Schools, Australian Government Publishing Service, Canberra.

DEMAILLY, L. (1991),
  Le collège : crise, mythes et métiers, PUL, Lille.

GALE, T. (1994),
  "Beyond caricature: Exploring theories of educational policy", *The Australian Educational Researcher*, Vol. 21, No. 2, pp. 1-12.

GONCZI, A., HAGER, P. and OLIVE, L. (1990),
  Establishing Competency-based Standards in the Professions, Australian Government Publishing Service, Canberra.

GOODSON, I. and MARSH, C. (1997),
Studying School Subjects – A Guide, Falmer Press, London.

GREEN, A. (1997),
"Education and state formation in Europe and Asia", in K. Kennedy (ed.), *Citizenship Education and the Modern State*, Falmer Press, London, pp. 9-26.

HAGER, P. (1994),
"Is there a cogent philosophical argument against competency standards?", *Australian Journal of Education*, Vol. 38(1), pp. 3-18.

HAGER, P. and BUTLER, J. (1994),
"Two paradigms of assessment", Paper presented at the Annual Conference of the Australian Association for Research in Education, University of Newcastle, 27 November-1 December.

HEYWOOD, L.H., GONCZI, A. and HAGER, P. (1992),
A Guide to Development of Competency Standards for Professions, Australian Government Publishing Service, Canberra.

ILLICH, I. (1971),
Deschooling Society, Harper and Row, New York.

KENNEDY, K. (1993),
"National curriculum policy development in Australia: A review and analysis of Commonwealth government involvement in the school curriculum", in K. Kennedy, O. Watts and G. McDonald (eds.), *Citizenship Education for a New Age*, pp. 7-18.

KENNEDY, K. and MILLS, G. (1996),
"Curriculum policy developments in the Asian-Pacific region: A cross-country analysis", Paper presented at the 20th Annual Conference of the Pacific Circle Consortium, Sydney, 12-15 May.

KENNEDY, K., WATTS, O. and McDONALD, G. (1993),
Citizenship Education for a New Age, University of Southern Queensland Press, Toowoomba.

LAI, W. (1995),
"Aspects of curriculum reform in the People's Republic of China. Project Report No. 1", Paper prepared for the Schooling for the Twenty-first Century Project.

LEWIN, K. (1948),
Resolving Social Conflicts, Harper, New York.

MENDRAS, H. (1983),
Le changement social, Armand Colin, Paris.

MILLS, G. (1995),
"Schooling for the twenty-first century: Can we change course before its too late?", Paper presented at the 19th Annual Meeting of the Pacific Circle Consortium, Vancouver, 21-25 April.

MORRIS, P. (1996),
The Hong Kong School Curriculum: Development, Issues and Policy, Hong Kong University Press, Hong Kong (China).

NONAKA, I. and TAKEUCHI, H. (1995),
   The Knowledge-creating Company: How Japanese Companies Create the Dynamics of Innovation, Oxford University Press, Oxford.

OECD (1996),
   Lifelong Learning for All, Paris.

OECD (1998),
   Redefining Tertiary Education, Paris.

PAPADOPOULOS, G. (1994),
   Education 1960-1990: The OECD Perspective, OECD, Paris.

PEDDIE, R. (1995),
   "Culture and economic change: The New Zealand School Curriculum", in D. Carter and M. O'Neill (eds.), *Case Studies in Educational Change: An International Perspective*, Falmer, London, pp. 146-156.

PERRENOUD, P. (1984),
   La fabrication de l'excellence scolaire, Droz, Geneva and Paris.

PRESTON, B. and KENNEDY, K. (1995),
   Issues and Principles for the Application of the Draft Competency Framework for Beginning Teachers to Initial Teacher Education, Report to the Working Party on Teacher Competencies, Department of Employment Education and Training, Canberra.

PRESTON, B. and WALKER, J. (1994),
   "Competency standards in the professions and higher education: A holistic approach", in C. Collins (ed.), *Competencies*, Australian College of Education, Canberra.

SERRES, M. (1991),
   Le Tiers Instruit, François Bourin, Paris.

SPERBER, D. (1996),
   La contagion des idées, Éditions Odile Jacob, Paris.

WALKER, J. (1993),
   "Competency-based standards in teaching: A general rationale and conceptual approach", *Agenda Papers: Issues Arising from "Australia's Teachers: An Agenda for the Next Decade"*, School's Council, Australian Government Publishing Service, Canberra.

WATZLAWICK, P., WEAKLAND, J.H. and FISCH, R. (1988),
   Change. Principles of Problem Formation and Problem Resolution, Norton, New York.

OECD 1999

OECD PUBLICATIONS, 2, rue André-Pascal, 75775 PARIS CEDEX 16
PRINTED IN FRANCE
(96 1999 02 1 P) ISBN 92-64-17021-9 – 50545 1999